MW00620769

ACTION REALISM

ACTION REALISM

The Art of Action

Lawrence Ribeiro

FIRST EDITION, OCTOBER 2018

Copyright © 2018 by Lawrence Ribeiro

All rights reserved.
No part of this book may be reproduced or utilized in any form or by any means, electronic or mechanical, including photocopying, recording, or by any information storage and retrieval system, without permission in writing from the publisher.
For information: www.lawrenceribeiro.com

ISBN: 978-0-692-17510-1

For all those people who have doubted themselves, this book is for you.

Contents

PART 3 – THE BUSINESS

Special Thanks

Johanna Magnusson, Rachel Rausch, Bill Leaman, Anthony Delongis, Roberto Schaeffer, Larry Parker, CML/Geoff Boyle, Steve Hart, Val Dauksts, Kim Bernhard, Kaelem Cahill, Mako Kowaii, William Devital, Ron Haviv, Gary Powell, Vic Armstrong, Bruce Logan, Jeremy Timmins, Antal Kalik, Jef Groff, Sean Douglas, Caleb Deschanel, Eric Brodeur, Bob Beemer, Philippe Paget, D. Chris Smith, Eric Kowal, Ken Norris, Jason Myres, D.W. Plance, James Mathers, Ron Fischer, Brian Pohl, Tom Harper, Vilmos Zsigmond, Simon Longmore, Pete Antico, Mark Lonsdale, Ian Eyre, Cole McKay, Jonathan King, Gareth Smith, Harry Yoon, Fletcher Murray, Harry Betke, Thomas Myrdahl, Eric Sherman, Ira Tiffen, Spice Williams-Crosby, Bob Brown, John Kreng, Chris Bangle, Jeff Habberstad, Susan Vishmid, Eric Grabowski, Sebastien Stella, Lester Mordue, Mehdi Ranji, Andrew Giles, Craig Yanagi, Paul Thomas, Mark Tungate, Paula Fairfield, Andrew Canter, Shane Hurlbut, Joan Webb, Company 3, Mike Chiado, Jackie Lee, Cindy Corona, Doug Trumbull, Mark H. Weingartner, Steve Laszlo, Dan Kneece, Mark Filippo, Ronald Talley, Stewart Lee Beck, Mandell Winter, Guillaume Briot, Eduardo Quintino, Dr. Ferdinand Froning, Rick Pearson, Paulo Sellitti, Douglas Knapp, Stephen Harvey, James Mathers, J.J. Perry, Keanu Reeves, Jon Blattmacher, Sabrina Allaria, John Roumelis…

Couldn't have done it without:

Howard Wexler, Lane Leavitt, Alex Nicolson, David McCullough, Garrett Warren, Ray Zimmerman, Andy Armstrong and Karin Chien.

Studying

When reading this book, it is important to fully understand the technical jargon being used, as the industry relies on specific meanings when using certain words. To make the most of the material presented below, I encourage you to look up any ambiguous or confusing terminology in the dictionary before proceeding. Sometimes knowing a word's etymology triggers new understandings.

Disclaimer

This book is offered for educational purposes *only*. The information provided in this book is designed to offer information relating to the subjects discussed herein. The author is not an expert in the field of stunts or any other extreme or dangerous activities.

This book is not meant to be used, nor should it be used, as an instructional guide for the activities described herein. The author is not responsible and disclaims any responsibility or liability for any and all loss, injury, or death that may result from any person(s) attempting to engage in any of the activities described. References are provided for informational purposes only and do not constitute the author's endorsement of any website or any other source, or of any of the activities described therein.

Purpose

When I was six, I liked to take different paths home every day. One day, I took the "creek way." Like most Canadian kids, as I walked, I would try to break all the ice along the bank of the creek so as to not get a "soaker." That particular day, under a bridge, I fell into the ice. No one could hear me scream because of the noise from the traffic above. I had no choice but to get myself out. I ran home soaking wet and freezing.

Hollywood is kind of like that. You need to know how to pull yourself out of the ice and not only survive, but thrive. Ultimately, you are on your own.
This book is meant as a guide. It contains some of my own creative insights into new techniques, as well as some thoughts on the pitfalls of "the business."

Certain chapters will discuss concepts that are meant to change the final product you produce. The end goal? Raw, unleashed, visceral imagery that enthralls the viewer.

This text is geared toward action filming and second unit, indie films and branded content, but it will refer to classical cinematography elements as well as cutting-edge principles.

In Hollywood, we have some long-standing traditions in terms of movie-making. I will explain the status quo and then provide solutions.

Because of this, the following people, after reading this book, will have more options when making creative decisions:

- producers
- directors

- DPs (directors of photography)/cinematographers
- UPMs (unit production managers)
- line producers
- brands / manufacturers
- creative /art directors
- young people
- veterans
- executive producers
- managing directors
- executive creative directors
- inventors/innovators
- independent filmmakers
- stunt people
- second unit directors
- stunt coordinators
- branding agencies
- accounts

You'll be educated in the arts, as you need to know the rules before you can break them.

The business is changing so fast, and realistically; even the powers that be and talking heads don't know the answers. This book will prepare you for the future.

There are plenty of other books out there that will offer technical opinions, but all you will get is more regurgitated material. However, basics are key, and they can be learned from some schooling, mentoring or standardized textbooks.

These are exciting times. For the first time, the System, the Establishment, status quo, whatever you want to call it, can be bypassed. With the price of equipment coming down and social media thriving as a vehicle for sharing work, you are in a position to do something great!

This book will offer something for bigger-budget shoots, too. I approached the top people in their respective fields, successful professionals with 25-40 years of experience. You have viewed and loved their work. I shared some of my techniques, concepts, and theories with these well-respected artists with the idea of getting feedback. This book is the accumulation of that.

You, the artist, have unlimited potential to create, and I'm here to assist you with that…

Introduction

It started one night when my face lay in the mud…
waiting for the police to leave. I had just been in a car
chase with a biker from a local chapter. It was a night
right out of a Hollywood movie, down to the scene
where the hero's car gets rammed side by side from
his rival.

Once we "stopped", he approached me with a tire
iron, which made me even madder.

My father knew that this was how I was living my life.
Something would happen every weekend. He was dying
of cancer, but he wanted me to live. He gave me
money to leave, get out of my hometown. Ten days
after his passing, I was in a conflict zone. I finally felt
at "home." The chaos felt normal.

My thrill-seeking continued to escalate. I found
myself in jungles, working outside skyscrapers and
Heli-logging in British Columbia. All these dangerous,
exciting experiences, which had also allowed me to
explore foreign cultures, set me up pretty well for the
stunt world. In comparison to my younger days,
action/second unit was a piece of cake. The stuff I
had been doing before was real shit that didn't get
second takes.

What I would like to share with you is my *point of view.*

We're in an exciting and tumultuous time here in
Hollywood. Many innovations to the business, artistry
and technologies have reshaped the "biz" in recent
years, both for better and for worse.

Some may say the Canon 5D changed how we shoot.
I've heard people point the finger at the writers'
strike, or some attribute it to the events of 9/11.

Now, we have algorithms dictating artistry in tent-pole movies and the studio system.

Obviously, numbers play a big role on how a movie is made, but introducing math is a sign that we're on the way out. The bean counters of the studios may disagree... that is their right. Even that has changed. Before, people went up the ranks starting from the bottom, and by the time they made it to the top, they knew most facets of the business. Now, they are hired out of ivy-league business schools, and their "artistic" talents consist of monitoring Google analytics, subscriptions, "likes", "followers" and YouTube hits.

Netflix truly is a game changer. It is creating content at break-neck speed. But Netflix too relies on analytics. I dare say that its quality of content has weakened since 2016, but you do see other countries, particularly Korea and Japan, getting in the Netflix game and bringing impressive films to western audiences.

Google's presence in L.A., and with Facebook not too far behind, speaks to what lies ahead. They've got the bucks!

Hulu, Apple and Amazon are all in the game. Most agencies and brands are on this path too. It's a shame.

I may have painted a picture of doom and gloom, but the purveyors of chaos do that 24/7. However, I would like to introduce certain things that can manifest a different final result, as a finished artistic piece/product.

Let's use hockey as an example. In the NHL lockout of 2004-2005, a meaningful change took place that distinctly altered the game. They took out the red line, the centerline. This single difference changed the game forever... it made it faster. The big bad lumbering hockey players could not keep up. Another change was introduced: a rule against hooking (holding back people with a hockey stick). The big players in the past were strong enough to pull another player back to slow him down. Suddenly, in 2005, the game became all about speed. Prior to the rule change, the average player was over 6'4" and weighed 240 pounds before putting on his ice skates. Obviously there were exceptions. But by and large, these were football linebackers on ice. It made for some great highlights each night, let me tell you! I am certain that some of these guys had stamps on their lockers, like World War II fighter pilots, of "enemies" they had taken out.

Anyhow, now the players range from 180 to 200 pounds. Their style of play is completely different in that weight class. Coaches created new strategies, players used different techniques, and the game began to be played differently. Now, NHL teams are introducing figure-skating coaches because players are catching up, and they have to be able to turn around or get out of the way for an incoming 200-pound missile or be lighter on their feet. This is all from *one* rule change…

Similarly, the film business is roughly a hundred years old, and there have been a lot of fantastic creations long before I came along. I want to introduce a different way of looking at certain factors, time periods and practices. Further, I will take some agreed-upon beliefs to a more basic form.

Some of these things are so deeply rooted that in some cases, people can't think around them, or don't question them, or don't alter them for politics' sake. I understand this all too well.

For almost 2,000 years, experienced sailors saw monsters out at sea. It wasn't until recently that we discovered what those monsters were. The sailors of ancient Phoenicia, along with Portuguese and Spanish conquistadors, and members of the British royal navy all saw "monsters." What they actually saw was a sperm whale having lunch! You see, the sperm whale catches his prey, the squid, in the deep ocean where the squid lives. However, the whale is an air-breather, so he has to fight the squid all the way to the surface to eat it. The squid fights him all the way up. It's amazing when a mystery is resolved.

If it weren't for the likes of Jacques Cousteau or even James Cameron with his research and fascination with the Titanic, these discoveries may never had been made. These mysteries would not have been solved.

What about the Catholic Church in medieval times predicting the eclipse and using that knowledge to fool their followers into believing that it could control the sun? There is no mystery now.

Where mysteries *were* planted was in the education system, by the robber barons.* They were instrumental in pushing the education system to focus on what they thought the public "should" have been learning, rather than on what was needed to have a full and meaningful life. In the 1950s, semantics were used to change the meaning of words for the purpose of manipulating the language. Another phase was the political correctness movement that started in the 1990s – another means of manipulating the language. This compounded to bring us to our current state, where we are constantly bombarded with images of

---

* A robber baron is an American tycoon, a person who has become rich through ruthless and unscrupulous business practices, particularly in the nineteenth century.

brands and corporations. As a result, we are losing our ability to think for ourselves! Our current society is dumbed-down with just one outcome: forcing you to consume, to buy products.

One of my most recent projects was a car chase, and all I had was a camera and a strap. That's it. If Roger Deakins had a flashlight, a bed sheet, some Vaseline and daylight... I'm pretty convinced he could make something amazing. Even with a smart phone. He can think with it. Remember Keanu Reeves – Baba Yaga, the boogeyman killer...all he had was a pencil – a *fucken* pencil!

Based on the idea that we are guided by "The Academy of Motion Picture Arts *and* Sciences," this book will balance both so as to keep things in check. Theory and practice must exist hand-in-hand for complete understanding.

The ideas I have laid out in the following chapters were worked out in cooperation with many great people – top cinematographers, stunt coordinators, second unit directors, editors, sound designers and artists of different media. You can't look at the future without a good look at the past, especially with classically trained eyes.

Some things in this book you may be very familiar with, and some not. What I am offering is a new combination, with introductions to different concepts and practices. I offer a new paradigm of the process. By using these principles, you will be able to continue to create by finding a style or changing it according to what *you* want to introduce.

Maybe you'll put the red line back in?

What is Action Realism?

Action Realism encompasses creating speed - dynamic, visceral images - by integrating several areas: production design, locations (scouting), shooting of the image, editing, action design with or without the camera, sound design, music and lastly incorporating culture.

My emphasis is on location scouting, production design, and eliminating the camera "bottleneck". Most of you are not shooting with *Fast & Furious* budgets that allow 12-16 camera setups, so "camera bottleneck" is key. What does that mean? Consider what can you "fit" in the image and still have it be exciting, even if you have only one camera! I often rely on the location to be the catalyst, to give it that dynamic *look, feel* or *speed*. Your shooting environment - the location and production design - is integral to creating that *illusion* of speed.

A common action is to edit the hell out of something to get *speed*. Keep in mind, speed doesn't always have to be created in post. There may be something else you can use in the production design, choreography, or camera movement to create speed in camera. In other words, don't rely on just one department. Once you understand the components of what makes up Action Realism, no matter if your budget is small or big, you can maximize the departments and the elements you do have.

My knowledge has been obtained by putting in my 10,000 hours, but most importantly by making my "10,000" mistakes. In addition, I've traveled the globe, scouted diverse environments, and visited the practical locations where the best action sequences have been filmed, in order to break down exactly how they integrated the landscape, the location, the camera angles, the equipment, the talent. I have shot a lot of previz (previsualization) and put myself in risky positions to get *that* image. I've worked on developing a point of view in order to innovate new equipment and technology to obtain images "outside of the box". As a result, I've arrived at one of the most efficient ways to create action.

I'm not here to prove anything to anybody. What I want is to give the reader, perhaps someone who has some filmmaking basics, the ability to create visceral and dynamic images, cost-effectively!

It doesn't matter if you are a veteran producer or a young Youtuber. This book is designed to give you a point of view to see *your own strengths.* This book encourages you to apply your strengths and guides you to think for yourself as an artist or filmmaker. Opinion leaders, media, advertising, and marketing departments work hard to influence your opinions of what you should or should not do (or, buy). My role is to help you develop a keen sense of yourself and your abilities. As a result, a director, account manager, creative director, production manager or cinematographer, etc., reading this book will also get a better idea of how to put together a more exciting project while becoming more cost-effective.

Lastly, some of my favorite movies are not VFX heavy by any means. *Being There, Apocalypse Now, Goodfellas, Shawshank Redemption, The Natural, Once Upon a Time in the West,* and of course the first three *Bourne* movies and *MadMax: Fury Road* are not only great action films, but they are masterpieces in their own right. VFX is a department that is here to stay and is certainly an important cog in the machine, but that is not why this book was written. This book was written for two reasons: to live life while developing your *own* point of view and to bring back realism - Action Realism.

Part 1
Prep/Basics

The Basics

You are the viewer, and you are the creator.

You need to *see* with your eyes before you can create. You will be seeing what hopefully or eventually the audience will see.

Hone this skill by training your eyes with a finely tuned instrument – a toilet paper roll. Yes, a toilet paper roll.

What you are trying to do with this finely tuned "instrument" is train your eyes to be discriminating. Differentiating one thing from another gives clarity on a subject. At pretty much any given moment, there are thousands of things in your range of sight, probably millions if you count the details. It's really the *details* that you need to be aware of.

A couple of things to keep in mind:

1) If you are shooting action, things, or objects, can move extremely fast, almost to the point of no control. If you can't see them at a slower speed, you are surely not going to see them at a faster speed.

2) Making the shot *interesting* is completely up to you, as you are the artist. So is moving the story forward. I will talk more about this later.

3) Encompassing culture. This is important enough to have its own chapter.

Try this exercise for five minutes: look at things in the room you are in right now. Look at a picture, a poster, a desk, whatever surrounds you, with the toilet paper roll. You will start noticing little details, like the font that was used, a nick on the desk or a stray hair. These are specific details. Spend a full five minutes doing this, or more if you'd like. You might find it rather engrossing.

When using the toilet paper roll to look at the world begins feeling routine or automatic, take it to the next step. Are you ready? Use a paper towel roll... You will start seeing the curves of a font that the stray hair had been partly in the sun, etc.

I did this for about a year or so before one day, while I was looking at a parking sign (of all things!) I saw seven shots in a matter of seconds. It just raced through my mind. Every little detail was right there in front of me, and I could see each one. I knew I could imbue these details with life with the use of a camera. Now, noticing these things is second nature to me, and every waking second I see minute details.

As a filmmaker or observer, when you notice the little things, you also begin being able to predict what comes next, for example a muscle flexing right before someone gets up from a chair. Do they push more with one hand than the other? Doug Knapp, a veteran camera operator, drew my attention to that one when I was starting out.

You might see someone is right-handed, but has a tendency to use their left hand for specific actions. There's a good chance that they had been left-handed earlier in life, and their parents or teachers conditioned them to use their right hand. That was very common in the past.

My mentor had driven down his local road for many years knowing every nook and cranny, so to speak, from traffic patterns to the lighting, etc. Even though it was far away, he could time a shot of a plane landing in LAX from ten miles away! He would continually look forward day after day, month after month, and year after year. It may seem like a waste a time, but the truth of the matter is what else do you do when you are looking forward? However, I see this as a discipline, and that is a mark of a professional.

This point I'm making is a skill you will need to develop to the point where it becomes unconscious and that you have even made a mental note of such details. I suspect this is one of the reasons cinematographers are generally quiet… they are making mental notes of the things they see around them.

But watching the world doesn't have to be boring! You can be at the supermarket checking out a beautiful person… is she confident? It'll show in her walk. Does she know that she's turning heads? Or is she trying to get back to the office or home to her family?

Or some meathead at the gym. You know the guy who puts on 10-45 pound weights, then leaves the device and makes sure to flex as he passes the mirror?

Or maybe you are in the wrong neighborhood, and you see some gangbanger type walking with that particular "badass" walk. When a guy has done some hard time or has been in the special forces and has seen a lot of action, you can tell by the way he looks at you or looks *through* you.

If you are ever in a position to see a ballerina who was classically trained in Russia, you will surely see years of disciplined training right in her body, her instrument. She'll move with such grace and elegance that it will be like watching a painting in motion.

I have several friends who are performers in Cirque du Soleil, and the first part of their contract is to spend three to four months rehearsing in Montreal, and then another two to four months rehearsing on location, depending on the level of difficulty. This is well after they have already become consummate professionals in their respective disciplines. Their movements are masterful with timing and fluidity, but that is born of practice and hard work. Their participation in this moving art has been years in the making.

Some years back, a friend of mine was in a fight in Thailand for ESPN. It turns out that at the last minute, the other fighter backed out, and had to be replaced by this guy from a rural village in the jungle. My friend was very humble, and I recall him telling me that during the fight, he saw an "opening." He said punches and kicks were coming so fast, but if he had taken advantage of this opening, it would have been like "kicking a pumpkin." So he delayed his kick for a fraction of the second, because otherwise, he felt he would've killed his opponent. This was a responsibility issue.

His eyes were trained in such a way to see things as ours are not. This epitomizes hand-eye coordination which has been honed by years of training.

Recently, I have been working with a martial artist and gun specialist. He trains Mossad and other special forces and has been getting into the movie game. During one exercise, I saw him take down four professional fighters in the less than three seconds. You don't even realize what is happening, and he has already taken them out!

Let's say you are shooting or directing some stunt people, their movements have to be *sold*, meaning they have to be physically believable on camera. Whereas an actor has to be believable on an emotional level. These two different disciplines and perspectives, when combined, result in a better finished product. Understanding both will give you more options to create!

In one of the last sequences of *Shooter* with Mark Wahlberg, the house is blown up, and as that is happening, he walks by as Markie Mark in the foreground. It could have been a stunt double, but because there is no second house to blow up, that take was used. You see the character was a disciplined military individual. Military men usually stand erect, because that is how they have spent years being trained to stand. For that one split moment, Mr. Wahlberg went out of character, and that was in the shot. The camera doesn't lie.

If you watch fight sequences now and compare them to the sequences of 30-40 years ago, you can hardly believe it. Now, the stunt/fight coordinator's responsibility is to get the stunt people to sell it on *every* level and still move the story forward. However, in the States, they are not given much time, compared to Hong Kong, for example, where they may spend a month on a single fight!

Note: There are different time allowances for commercials (branded content), television and movies. It's the nature of the beast.

Remember, it's all in the details…

Knowledge by Observation

There are the arts and sciences. Then there is observation.

What is observation, and how is this used? Or, more importantly, how can this be used by people in the film or advertising industries?

I've always been fascinated with Native American mythology & culture, and the powers of observation that have been passed on over generations. To this day, the U.S. military uses Native American trackers, despite the ungodly amounts of money allotted for weapons and technology that were meant to replace "the human factor." Supposedly, trackers are the way of the past. But what is it that they have, or should I say, that the average military-trained individual does not?

Trackers, Native Americans and cowboys who lived out in the plains, could read the land, look at the sky, blue as can be, and were more accurate than the modern-day weather man. Why is that?

There are military units that have basic training so as to not be detected by the enemy, skills like not breaking branches or scraping bark, being quiet, or if there is snow, swishing away footprints, etc.

These advanced military skills are generally passed down by the wisdom of others, and the Native Americans were the masters of these skills, which they developed well before the "civilized" man came around. Unfortunately, "modern" times have diminished these skills.

I always thought the stories of the Vedic hymns (*The Four Vedas*) were written along the same pattern. It is believed that each of those stories was passed down from generation to generation. Eventually, they sort of forgot the whole story, and as a result, the *Vedas* were written for further generations.

The long and short of it, people, is that if you don't use it, you'll lose it.

I have spent a lot of time in various locales where I met people who knew the land (the bush) and environment better than I did, but they were able to share with me. For example, if you are consumed by the forest and can't orient yourself, get to a higher vantage point and look down to assess the surroundings. Most of the time, there will be this streak of trees where the color of leaves will be distinctively different from the rest of trees in the area. This is a sign of disturbed soil, which is usually a trail, a creek or an old logging road.

Somebody had to observe this before they could share it.

What I'm getting at is developing your ability to *observe*. If you were to do an observation drill, you will see that your skills have actually been lost.

For example, in a non-creepy fashion, look at someone. *Really* look at them. In the position that they are in *at that given moment*. What do you see? Do you actually see both ears? Don't assume they have both ears. Or even one ear. Do you *actually* see an ear, or is it covered by hair? This is key.

Look at another part of the body: look at their hands. Do you see *all* the fingers? Or just some fingers? Maybe even partial fingers?

The minor details can be the difference between making something interesting and not.

When you are on set, and there are various people doing their thing or checking the equipment themselves, this kind of thing, developing this skill can possibly save your life, because when you are in the arena of stunts, it can be a life or death situation! But it is also important simply for getting that shot you intended to get.

There are going to be other people doing their jobs, but even myself, if I'm using a harness aka jerk vest (please Google an image of this) from someone else, and I don't know the background of it, or has it been lying in the sun, I need to observe it for frayed stitching etc. and make a determination as to whether I want to use it.

Even more importantly, use your powers of observation to account for personalities. Stunts should always be performed with the appropriate safety precautions, obviously. However, I don't trust safety precautions as the last line of defense from getting hurt. First, I must see and observe who is in the vicinity and who is *causing* trouble. Sometimes it's subtle, but sometimes it is not. Have you ever spoken to someone, and you felt slimed, or not quite good about yourself afterwards?

In second unit/action, things can be intense, and there's a lot of testosterone and the odd shoe throwing. Do you think that might throw you off your game? Do you see people getting hurt after seeing someone being difficult with someone else, or being shouted at, or simply feeling like shit?

It's best to stay away from people who can throw off your A-game, if possible, or at least be aware of how they operate. If the set is running right, and the stunt coordinator knows what they're doing, and more importantly takes pride in their set, then you should be OK.

I can recall being on a shoot with a buddy where we were essentially being circled by a drifting car while shooting. The stunt coordinator put himself in the situation first. He took responsibility and felt out the situation and the talent behind the wheel before letting anyone else put themselves at risk.

Other times I heard him speaking... "that would not happen on *my* set." He owns it, and that is professionalism in my eyes. It's his name on the line if someone gets hurt. How is your confidence after seeing or hearing something like that?

Moreover, your powers of observation *enhance* the image quality of what you are seeing. *Your responsibility is to get the shot.* Do you think your skills will develop more after doing an observation drill? Because after all, the final product is for the *audience*. Further, you can make the images better, or in the case of action, more dynamic and visceral.

Fine artist and painter schools still use the above drill. It's standard operating procedure.

In summary, take responsibility for the space around you so that you or somebody else doesn't get hurt or killed. Use observation both to protect yourself and those around you, *and* to increase your ability to enhance the image.

Talent – Gauging It

If there is one thing you need to remember after reading this book, it is this: you have to gauge talent. More people get hurt or killed in second unit/stunts than any other department in the film industry.

I've been drilled on it, but by and large I have been in an environment where a lot of this is done for me, so to speak.

What I will say right off the bat is that there is a *huge* difference between somebody who is really good at something and somebody who is a world champion. The discipline, skill and clarity of mind required to become a world champion take a lot of time and effort to achieve.

You may want to watch out for new guys who talk too much, telling stories rather than listening. There's a big difference between that and someone who has habitually worked his skills to the point where the adrenaline doesn't affect them… as much.

Further, in the low-budget world, projects don't always use a stunt coordinator due to budget constraints. Without a stunt coordinator, you learn whether a "stuntman" was lying very quickly. In one case, someone claimed that he had been taking martials arts for five years. It turns out he had been taking random classes at 24-Hour Fitness, and none of this training had been in front of a camera, which is a vital step in performing/learning. This mistake cost the project more time and money than an A-list or veteran stuntman who could have knocked it out in no-time.

Having experienced people around doing car/bike stunts, high falls, fire burns, wire work, etc. allows us to have a reference point. There's a guy or gal out there who's tougher, faster, crazier, more skilled, agile or experienced than you. Then you also have single stunt performers versus married with kids, etc, these are all considerations.

I can recall doing a high fall, testing camera equipment for impact. I was pretty impressed with myself. After I did the jumps, I was just talking to some stunt buddies, and one of them mentioned that Garrett Warren had done a 150-foot jump with a camera. Actually, they mentioned two other stories about Garrett, and I thought they were messing with me. He's one of Hollywood's biggest badasses.

Garrett is not only one of the top stunt coordinators on the planet, he knows camera technologies really well and knows what he's looking for in terms of the upcoming shoot/shot. When I first met him, we were going over some equipment, and I realized that this guy was two steps ahead of me; and I decided to keep my mouth shut. It was a good kick in the pants. Garrett's ability to gauge talent was obviously much higher than mine, but that is not to say that I am not observing what is going on or learning from him.

Another stunt coordinator I know, William Devital, was going over some shots that I was doing and said he knew I was a stuntman based on some photos from set that I had showed him. I reiterated that I was not a stuntman. However, I do have a lot of nerve and want to add to the shot. He told me about a shoot where he sat in the passenger seat, and when the car flipped, in midair, he pushed a camera through the windshield for an effect. I later looked at a reel where he had a shot of climbing under a moving train and climbing out. It was amazing. You wouldn't be allowed to do this in the U.S.

Just remember there's a guy or a gal out there with a lot more nerve than you.

With YouTube, Instagram, etc. it's even easier to see talent.

The stunt coordinator, as far as I'm concerned, is the last line of defense. The director and producer want that shot, and the stunt coordinator needs to step in and say "no," which is not as easy to do when you're talking to folks higher on the food chain. The director and producer have to find another way to do it, or find someone who can do it, or fire the stunt coordinator and get a monkey to say "yes." Different people choose different combinations of these options.

This is certainly not your responsibility, but you should be aware of it, because if someone gets hurt or killed, you will feel like shit. I don't care how tough you think you are; there will be a lot of teary-eyed people around.

Young men: these guys sometimes get *so* amped up that they don't actually hear what's being said! The adrenaline is pumping through them, which can be dangerous. They may duplicate you wrong, misstep, etc. and screw up. Meanwhile a veteran, or a family man, needs and wants to come home.

How each of them perceive the situation is completely different. However, the younger body can take more abuse. It has more "bounce," so to speak. When you are younger, you bounce and you get right up, as you get older, you get banged up, and it becomes harder to get up.

Stuntwomen: these gals are tough. There are certain luxuries that men have that women don't. For example, if women are falling down a set of stairs in an evening dress, they can't hide their protective gear as a man can. They usually have to be a body double for some young thin actress, so they can't beef up too much. You see women getting hit by a car, coming over the hood, then on the windshield, then onto the ground. Some of these gals would put my hockey buddies to shame!

One thing I don't like about the business is that stunt people do get shit on, a lot. There's no Oscar for them, yet no studio movie can be made without them. They train incessantly. I've seen multiple rehearsals of stunt people being thrown on the ground, day in and day out. It's a tough gig. If you don't pull it off, you'll get an earful e.g. "my grandmother can do better than that," "you are a dime a dozen" or my personal favorite: the shoe throwing.

Dealing with an A-list/veteran stunt person versus somebody starting out is a huge difference. I've worked with both, and you need to be aware of how different these two types of people are. Sort of you get what you pay for, but depending on the budget that may be all you have. I will tell you this; it still might be cheaper to pay for talent than deal with the problems you might get with a newbie.

I have put myself in risky situations plenty of times only to have the shot go limp because the newbie or young performer didn't get it right. Meanwhile, a top stunt guy can hit the mark, not much dialogue and right on the money, pretty much every time. Perhaps ask "does this work for you?"

Sometimes, with actors, it can take some time. It's no different for someone who is new to the stunt world. And as I mentioned before, they may have a background in fighting, but for the camera it's a whole different story.

Conversely, I have a personal friend who is one of the top stuntmen on the planet. I had gauged an hour plus for him to get the moves we needed for a fight sequence with another fighter. Ten minutes after he starts practicing, he comes up to me: "got it." And he had it.

More experience translates to looking better on camera. *The camera can be one of the most evil things for talent.* You have to try to make it as comfortable as you can for whoever is in the shot, especially if they are new or inexperienced in front of the camera.

There was this fellow I was shooting while he was skate boarding. He was perfect every time when the camera was off. As soon as the camera came on, he wiped out. Every single time. This can't be ignored!

What happens if it's a really dangerous shoot? There's *no* room for error.

You have to be prepared: get reels, talk to other people/productions to find out if your stunt person can really do what they say they can, etc. If they are not certain in their actions, you still have to get the shot, so you have to work with them to make sure it works.

Who do you want? Do you want someone who can get hurt, or even killed? Or do you want someone who makes you look good?

Stunts / Second Unit Department

Stunt people and the stunts department, if you will, is not like any other "department."

Each department has its own character and culture, and the stunt community is quite tight, more so than others, I feel. They are a very loyal group.

There are a few rumblings here and there, where you'll hear "that guy couldn't hold my lunch pail." I find this kind of amusing, but it exists. Usually from the old school guys. Politics in the stunt world can be pretty thick. Despite some of the idiosyncrasies of the industry, stunt people generally give support to their colleagues and participate in lots of activities that support certain charities and similar activities. They are very group-oriented. There are multiple associations for stunt people, and they have their own industry award: the Taurus Awards.

Personally, I've always been fascinated with the stunt community, as its members are very talented. Let's not forget, even though we don't "make" much movies in Los Angeles anymore, the city has the largest talent base of stunt people on the planet! These are world-class athletes, ex-Olympians, motorcycle/car champions, ex-fighters, etc. No shortage of amazing people and stories! I found, for the most part, the more talented someone is, the more humble they can be. Traveling and working around the world has allowed me to see a lot of talent. Each country can have its own skills and quirks...and there can be a lot of them!

We're sort of going through an evolution in L.A., and second unit/stunts is no different. I may be a little biased towards them, but I do see some things that are less than ideal. In some cases, they are taking matters into their own hands by creating their own content and productions.

There's a wide variance of backgrounds, as I mentioned briefly, which sort of gives it this carnie feeling. I can recall a veteran stunt coordinator who came from rodeos as a rodeo clown. He is one of the top stunt drivers in town, and he has broken his back twice. He's flipped more cars than you have bought fancy coffee drinks! Probably a background that is not too common anymore.

What I'm getting at, L.A. is very cyclical. Hollywood will keep trying similar formulas, but you need to set yourself apart. And with the inception of smaller cameras, tighter budgets, better talent, or more talent, it makes for an interesting melting pot.

In the 1950s and 60s, some of these fellows came from the military, diving, gymnastics, and rodeo/ranch background. I can recall having this conversation with the late Loren Janes about being the stunt driver/double for Steve McQueen in the movie *Bullitt*. Loren's background was that of a high diver! But during that time frame, as Loren says, "people were *learning* to drive. "Everybody was doing it."

Conversely, I recall talking to somebody from one of these outfits that use the Ultimate/Russian arm about how if you are not at least a world champion, you can forget it, in terms of being a camera car driver. This can be construed a couple of different ways. One, obviously, is that there is lot of talent here to choose from. Second, if you were in a smaller market, maybe you might have more of a chance, but may need be a national champion.

But I don't worry about these things, and neither should you. Come up with alternatives and *just do it*! This is part of the growing pains before you make it in the majors. You need to be creative, pull in favors, etc to make it happen. Learning these things when you don't have these luxuries is what really gives you that experience, because shit happens, and if you don't have an alternative... well, what do you do?

I've seen too many veterans pull things out of their asses and come out looking good. Using a cinematography analogy, famed Hungarian Cinematographers Vilmos Zsigmond and Laszlo Kovacs used to go over the border to have their film developed in another country as their country was being invaded by communists. These guys really wanted to make movies! There were no stores they could go to pick up certain equipment, so they used things like Vaseline and panty hose to create amazing cinematic effects. It was years later that they made it in Hollywood, but the bottom line is that they *never* gave up.

I have an extensive background in physics, and while I know people who are much more academic than myself, I could still figure it out. I would go to stores that sell the equipment, and start looking for cheaper alternatives or fabricate something from what's in my garage or at Home Depot. If you don't, it's your choice to succumb...

With stunts, particularly high falls, using cardboard boxes will suffice. Yes, I did say boxes. You can get those anywhere.

Somebody had to figure that out...

There has been some recognition in the technical achievement category of the Academy Awards of the likes stunt legend Vic Armstrong, and Yakima Canutt,

Hal Needham, and most recently Jackie Chan who was acknowledged a couple of years ago, which was nice. As well as Visual Effects pioneer Doug Trumbull of famed *2001: A Space Odyssey, Blade Runner* (the original).

These fellows have been instrumental in making your movie experience exciting!

David Watkin said in his Oscar acceptance speech for best cinematography for the film *Out of Africa*:

"A while ago I was sitting in a theater watching one of my movies next to a friend of mine who is a film director. And after about an hour he touched me on the arm and said, 'that's beautiful, you're very clever.' So I explained that it was a second-unit shot. So perhaps I think it's best if I point out that all of the flying material was shot by Peter Allwork, and the animal photography was Simon Trevor. I'm truly honored and very flattered, and thank you very much."

Classy guy. It's good to know that second unit can be a recognized department that contributes to the movie magic process.

The Jackie Chan Paradigm

Jackie has become very successful, which has afforded him some luxuries. He created a production company where people in his crew could practice together. When doing stunts, things are risky, fast and in some cases can be unexpected to the untrained eye.

With Jackie's company, he's able to pay people to practice weekly, like a tight military unit. This is valuable, as you learn to recognize not only your own, but also your colleagues' strengths and weaknesses.

You are only as good your weakest link.

A friend and I had constructed a process rig whereby we could shoot an actor who does not know how to ride a motorcycle. This took practice. Stunt innovator Lane Leavitt was behind the wheel and I was behind the camera. At one point, and I'm not sure how to describe this, it was as if I were cantilevering off the side of the speed rails (please Google - speed rails for car rigging). Just like sailors who are hanging off when the catamaran comes out of the water. It was dangerous. With Lane behind the wheel, I had complete confidence, because he's old enough not to need to show off, since if he jerked the rig wrong, I would be scraping my face on the ground. In the end, the attempted rig did not work to my satisfaction, but I learned lots from doing it.

Step two: have a "first AC," also known as a spotter. I positioned myself on the elevated area of the rig, but I always had someone hold me. I went through three stunt men to find the right one. The first guy bear hugged me whenever he thought I was about to wipe out. I was safe, but we blew the shot. The second guy felt the best way to remedy this was to pull me into the rig or push me out of the rig… while moving. Umm. No. The third guy was money. He was always there, but I didn't notice him. He was perfect. He allowed me to get the shot at high speeds, but had my back covered. You see, at that point, *that* position was the weakest link. I'm sure we could have improved the rig so as to get more speed, but we all know where we stood, and at any given point, we would be ready to get it set up and not worry that we couldn't pull it off. We trained to become a well-oiled machine for that particular apparatus/stunt.

The way I see this is that these drills are military in nature, which brings me to the next person: Mark Lonsdale.

Mark is ex-SAS (British Special Air Service) and has ascended Mount Everest three times. He certainly has my attention and respect. The way SAS soldiers train is not the same as in the U.S. military, though I'm sure there are special forces in the States that are similar, Delta, Navy SEALs, etc.

The SAS generally do simulation training that is compartmented so as to attain masterful proficiency before moving onto another segment. They have very high standards, and very few are ever recruited, only guys who have been in other armed forces are invited. Training may take a couple of years before they go on missions. I'll assure you of this much: there is no weak link at that point, and they would *never* let down their brother or mate.

Mark and I were talking about altitudes and standard operating procedure for ascending. What stood out for me was when he said, "at this altitude we do this, we drink this, and do this… and if this doesn't occur, we do this." That was long and short of it. There was no doubt in mind that he *knows what to do* at any given moment.

Certainty is key, and you *must have predictability*. When you train or shoot with somebody regularly, you know their strengths and weaknesses, especially with stunts or missions, as there is no room for error.

That's why we can cover each other's butt: you drill it over and over so you know it cold....

Simulation Training

Due to the speed and the nature of stunts and my overall point of view (shooting with the intent of making the images visceral or dynamic), I have come up with some exercises.

Scenarios, locales, speeds and context of the story will dictate how I train. Sometimes you just need a supply of guts, sometimes you need to overcome your fears, but the truth of the matter is that my feet rarely touch the ground when shooting. It's more mental than physical, because a few close calls can throw you off your game.

I was talking to one of the premiere Parkour/Freerunning guys in L.A. and he was telling me that on the set, you don't always get a chance to practice, so that when you finally come home it takes a while to get back in the swing of things.

How I will prep is different than how first (main) unit will prep. Obviously, the camera, lenses, workflow need to be covered, so that all the bugs have been worked out so as to not have any surprises when principal shooting starts.

Let's go over a few scenarios.

Let's assume you are going to the mountains to shoot. You need to know what the elevation is. Is it 3,000-5,000 feet or is it 8,000+? You will need to train differently depending on the answer to that question. Do you live at sea level, or do you reside in Colorado with most of the Ironman athletes?

Are you going to the desert... in the summer? That will take a toll on you if you are not used to it. It takes time to adjust. If you are getting work in the majors, you have to bring your A-game. B-list, independent work can sometimes be a bit of a free-for-all.

Another example, someone reached out to me for a shoot in which I had some interest, whereby I needed to rappel from a helicopter while shooting. That's a tough shot as it is.

Let's explore this for a second. Will the blades be turning? Rotor wash* is a big deal. Is there a budget to have somebody at the bottom to control the rappel so that I can just concentrate on shooting? If the blades are on, can they hear me and can I hear them? What time of day are we shooting, at the beginning of the day when we are fresh, or at the end of the day with "golden hour?" Will my colleagues be fresh too? *I can only assume the worst and train for that.* Does the guy at the bottom know what he's doing? If not, I may not sleep too well the night before. Trust is a big issue. Actually, the whole business is based on trust. The decision process is based on precise questions to the production manager or producer, consulting with colleagues, and instinct. In the end, I decided to pass on this opportunity.

But I do have a fair share of experience with helicopters, and I will share a skill that I have developed based on it…

I have spent some time Heli-logging (logging with helicopters) in the mountains in British Columbia. We used the Sikorski 64, a jet-propelled helicopter. It looks like a dragonfly. At the time, it was the fastest vertical climber on the planet. I have to admit, it was one of the most awesome pieces of machinery that I had seen!

---

* The air that is driven downwards from the propeller(s).

The logs we were extracting varied in terms of size, weight and quantity. For example, a log may pull a "cherry." One big log versus multiple logs, I believe I've seen up to eleven logs, thin ones on the same line. So, essentially, the pilot pulls upward and the logs are dangling. Then he comes downward to the landing zone (L.Z.). This is tricky, as the length has to be controlled, or some of the logs fall over the edge, and there are men down there. As soon as the helicopter releases the logs, a bulldozer type of machine, called a frontend loader, separates all of the logs. We would have to go in there, separate the cables a.k.a. "chokers."

All of this took 90 seconds…

Each cycle extracting from the "hill" to the L.Z. took 90 seconds. If you are at the bottom, it's easy to forget that time is passing, and the pilot of the S-64 sounds off the siren, which is usually a rude awakening. Moreover, the frontend loader is pulling the logs aggressively, and if you get caught next to the chokers, which are what we called the cables, they will break your leg or arm like a twig. We had two or three hospitalizations *per week*.

When you are on the "hill," it's a bit of a different animal.

Because the logs are just lying on the ground, there is debris everywhere from where they were fallen (cut down). As a result, you are not actually walking on land. You are, on average, three to five feet above the ground. This is the point of this story. I had to learn how to walk on the logs. We called it "bush legs." Essentially, you "walk" like an animal. You are springing from log to log.

Now, when the S-64 would come down, it was kind of tricky, because the rotor wash was so intense that tree limbs would fly up at you. So, you had to have three routes of escape. The hook, which doesn't really look like a hook by the way, is about the size of a small desk, and you connect the chokers to the hook. When you bolt out of there you give the pilot the command "clear." If you misstep, you are fucked, to put it mildly!

This experience, for me, has become invaluable for shooting, especially for fights. Your reflexes are *so* sharp, that I recall roughhousing with my buddies after I came out of camp, and they were all on the ground in a few seconds. Think about it like this… you are essentially sprinting ALL day on uneven ground, twelve hours a day *minimum,* and one mistake means you are taking a trip to the hospital.

Every so often, we had bomb threats just due to the nature of the business, which I didn't mind, because then I could relax for a little bit!

Everyone has experiences that they can draw from.

You'll have to make an examination of your skills to determine what you can use. You have to ask yourself if your skills can be used in the vein of movie making principles. That's the key.

One stunt/fight coordinators I've shot with, Steve Hart, had a great tip for shooting fighting. Two parts.

First was the idea of "happy feet." It means the two fighters get so excited they are a little out of sync: moving too quickly, over-embellishing what's going on. The second part was instead of 75% speed then 100%, we went 50% then 75%, and he asked them to "commit." *Really sell it.* From a camera operator's perspective this makes it easier to get the shots, and you can get in sync quite easily. Compound this with my "bush legs" from logging, and it was a piece of cake. Further, because of Steve's background as a fighter as well as his affinity for and understanding of cameras, it made for an efficient shoot. And it looked good too!

And this, in essence, is what this book is about: meshing well to make a more efficient product that is more visceral, if need be.

There are other things that you can enhance yourself with to be a better shooter. Go to the gym, ride motorcycles, do martial arts; essentially you can do anything you can think of that can improve your abilities for what you need to do better in terms of shooting various stunts.

I recall my buddy telling me that he used to see Haskell Wexler driving his Ferrari up the Hollywood Hills and more than likely Mulholland when it used to be a "race track" for people. This was the James Coburn and Steve McQueen era.

You need to keep your reflexes sharp.

One of the drills I use is working with half a ball, called a bosu ball. One side is curved and soft and gushy, and the other side is flat. The soft gushy part goes on the bottom. I stand on this and then I use two balls that I bounce against a wall or mirror and try to catch. The smaller the ball, the faster the response. You can slow it down by going further away from the wall or using bigger balls.

Sometimes I use red, green and blue balls, as these are the basic components of color. For variations, I will change the height or close one eye. The variations are endless. And you can't leave out footwork, because feet planting is a vital aspect, *especially* if there is any kind of risk. It doesn't matter if you are going down the stairs backwards or hanging from a helicopter.

Footwork is important. In some cases, you'll have a spotter, but you may not. There's a bit of a learning process to finding the ideal spotter.

Kicking the ball against the wall or doing some sort of soccer tricks is good for dexterity of footwork. You'll find weaknesses in both the upper and lower parts of your body. In either case, it's best to work on your weaknesses as opposed to working your strengths.

Note: in hockey, before the game, players limber up by horsing around with a small soccer ball. Europeans tend to be a bit better, having grown up with soccer, whereas most North Americans sports are played mostly with the upper body (basketball, baseball, etc.). It's probably one of the reasons European hockey players are generally better ice skaters, not to mention they have bigger rinks in Europe.

Don't neglect your footwork.

Some may or may not know that Bruce Lee was a champion in cha cha dancing (thanks, Mr. Kreng!). Obviously, he was known for his martials arts, but when dealing with choreography, footwork is the foundation.

Another interesting note: a strong neck is important. You don't want to be knocked out mid-shoot because of a weak neck.

As an example, here you are on the side of a cliff; you've rappelled down, and it's too high to have someone controlling the ropes from below. You are there to get a shot of a car coming over the cliff, and debris comes down, hits you on the head and knocks you out. How do you get back up? Sure, you can be pulled up, but that may fray the rope by weakening it, or the rope may snag, or something else could fall and hit you again, or worse, you could end up falling down.

These two components of footwork and strong neck are just examples of something to prepare for. Maybe you have developed these areas.

It's just something to think about, based on how *you* shoot and *your* particular skills.

There are multiple drills and exercises that I have developed for different scenarios, and I pick them out of my arsenal depending on the shoot. You'll have to discover what those are for *you*.

In closing, you generally need to be fit and ready, and if you are, and the opportunity arises, you'll be able to take advantage of it.

Biomechanics and Kinesiology

There are two things I've been preaching for some time: biomechanics and kinesiology.

Biomechanics: *the study of the application of mechanical laws and the action of forces to living structures.*

Kinesiology: *the study of the mechanics and anatomy of human muscles.*

I bring this up because movement is both how the body functions and how the eyes work in relation to the brain and what they see.

There are certain principles that are agreed-upon and proven scientifically to be pleasing to the eye. Like a dolly shot, a zoom is not natural, unless you are Steve Austin.*

There are certain principles in creating 3D, whether it's shot in production or done in post-production. The viewer is the recipient of that creation. When movies are rushed and the product suffers, I found most people over the age of 40 or who wore glasses, complained about 3D. It gets to the point that it actually created bad effects on the eyes and brain.

Just like movements of the eye and brain and their relationships, the body has similar parallels. Let me explain.

A sprinter generally looks like a football player rather than current Olympian Usain Bolt. Meanwhile, a long-distance runner looks like, well, a professional blood donor. Both move their legs, but *how* they move their legs and how they train those legs are

---

* The character in *The Six Million Dollar Man*, a television show from the 1970s.

different. The sprinter trains *each* part of the muscle. The long-distance runner may have another training protocol.

If two muscles are attached to each other (such as the buttock muscle and the hamstring) and do not have equal mobility, one will have potential injuries. Believe it or not, most people have this problem, but aren't even aware of it. Sprinters wouldn't be able to get to the speeds they reach if they were not.

The dancer Mikhail Baryshnikov, when he came to the U.S., was a true phenomenon. He had airtime before Michael Jordan's name even came up. The standards for ballet were so high at that time that there wasn't even anybody who danced in the same league as him in the States. Bruce Lee's speed is another example. If there was anything not functioning 100%, the body as a whole wouldn't function properly for him. All muscles have to be working independently.

So, how does this tie into filmmaking?

As an exercise, try walking with a glass full of water and not spilling it. Once you've become proficient with that, do it faster. Then do the drill climbing up some stairs, and then going down. You will notice that your legs will start operating differently. It's quite bizarre actually.

Ever seen models or pageant contestants training with a book on their heads? Would this manifest something unique? I think so: someone with an elegant and graceful walk. What about certain women in Africa or South America who carry things on their heads? Seems kind of odd to outsiders. However, they have their hands free, though their speed is limited.

Which brings us to equipment that we use in the film industry, such as the crane, ultimate/Russian arm, jib, Steadicam, camera stabilizers, etc. Each plays a role, none can do all, but they do serve a function well to capture an integral part of movie magic.

If you take a look at that versus what your body does, you'll see that we're not too far off with creating something similar *without* equipment.

There is a tribe of indigenous people in Northern Mexico (in Copper Canyon) called the Tarahumara Indians. What's kind of interesting about the Tarahumara is that they are considered some of the best ultra-runners on Earth.

Historically, the purpose of their running was not so much to be the best runner, but for *hunting*. Essentially, with certain game – deer or rabbits – they would just outlast the animal. Deer and rabbits can't sweat, so as a result, they would overheat and eventually just keel over while the hunters kept running. All the Tarahumara did was run after them. They could run 70-80 miles, no problem. One documentary I saw spoke of a runner who ran over 300 miles!

Now, they can't use our "modern" running techniques, as they are running barefoot or with sandals made out of old tires. High-tech! Their stride is different.

Modern shoes with elevated heels change the biomechanics of the body ever so slightly. Prior to the 1980s, where shoe manufacturers were not kings of marketing, people had less knee and hip problems than they do now, despite advancements in the medical arena. New doesn't necessarily make things better, but with carefully selected scientific and marketing claims, they tend to get more widespread recognition.

When observing Tarahumarian Indians standing still, I noticed their feet are duck-footed. Meaning, their feet aren't parallel, but pointed out. In the modern chiropractic world, that would mean their lower back is out. A podiatrist would correct that with shoe inserts. However, could it be that after generations of running and harsh environments, their bodies actually changed? I don't know, but the proof of the pudding is in the running.

Another exaggerated example of movement is a four-legged animal, specifically, the mountain lion or cougar.

When this predator is out hunting, it moves with *one* leg at a time, and if you happen to be tracked by one, you will notice that most of the time, it moves in *your* blind spot. Meaning, if it is being detected, it will stop immediately, as there are still three legs in contact with the ground. We don't have this option, but its sense of survival affords it the ability to be incredibly stealthy.

This is an exaggerated example, but I'm pointing out the fact of what movement can do in certain scenarios; and in this case in hunting. Don't rule out movement, as after all, what we are talking about is motion pictures. Biomechanics and kinesiology are another one of those things you need to continually observe, which brings me to the next pertinent subject, ergonomics.

Ergonomics

Ergonomics goes hand-in-glove with kinesiology and biomechanics. Essentially, you are the hand and the camera is the glove. Things can be awkward and happen really fast, and if you can't control the camera, *you can't get the shot.*

My emphasis on cameras is not necessarily for the image; it's more for whether I can get that shot with a particular camera. I said six years ago that this would be the decade of action films, and I believe that has come to fruition. There are a lot of options now, and in the not-too-distant future, many more coming.

I found with most departments in the studio system that they felt that their "thing" was the most important. All I know is that if it doesn't get captured, it won't be seen, regardless of quality, codec, etc.

I had this conversation with a producer, which turned into a little bit of debate. We had discussed the differences between first unit and second unit cameras in relation to qualities and capturing the image, specifically for second unit on *The Bourne Legacy* with Jeremy Renner during the motorcycle sequence at the end of the movie.

It's no easy feat to be pulling that sequence off in the first place.

Well, the first unit used the Arri Alexa, and for the inserts of the motorcycle, the Canon 5D Mark II. The quality of the insert shots was so poor that I actually thought it was filmed on a GoPro, especially in contrast to the amazing quality of the Alexa. When they shot that, they didn't have as many choices as they do now. This is not an issue anymore with the minicams. *Note: The technology is a bit dated but used for the purpose of this argument.*

The producer's viewpoint was that for second-unit images, if the camera is lower quality, this actually shocks the viewer, as the spectrum is so wide in terms of quality, which is a completely valid viewpoint.

We were talking about a shoot of me rappelling with the Sony F65, which is an amazing camera, but a bit of a tank at the time and a little awkward just to hold, never mind on the side of a cliff or mountain. I went over the dangers and concerns; I had different perspectives and eventually felt that we could come to an agreement. Now, five years later, we have many more options.

Further, these insert shots are generally less than a second. So, you have to weigh the factor of quality versus danger.

If the story is strong enough and the editing and sound design are well-executed, those shots are not as noticeable. I notice these things more than an average viewer due to my proximity to the talent/stunt, and I strive for perfection as all artisans in the industry do. But the truth of the matter is, I'm just a small cog in the wheel…

Another aspect of cameras is that the ideal weight is five to seven pounds, generally the weight of prosumer cameras, which we are coming very close to. Moreover, if the camera is well designed, then it may make the weight of the camera a little redundant.

There was a camera that was very popular back in the day, heavy but very balanced. It was made by a French company – the Éclair. I had a great conversation with Steve Weiss of Zacuto, and he said "if camera companies designed their cameras right…

they would put me out of business." Something to ponder…

There are certain things that I look for in camera – balance and weight, as *you don't want to fight the camera*, essentially. I rarely have both feet on the ground, nor am I pulling focus – *I am getting that shot, at all costs*. How nimble is the camera under duress? Having finger grips is crucial for me so I can manipulate it, sort of just flick it like a gunslinger.

I see a lot of fancy stuff that looks cool and modern, but if it doesn't function well, it's useless. More "stuff" on your camera doesn't necessarily make you a better filmmaker. It really comes down to you. You may have skills that make up for your camera's shortcomings or whatever. It doesn't matter.

To take this further, look at the tools that are out there that people use, for many hoursm throughout their daily grind – a garden blower, a chainsaw, semi-automatic weapons/rifles etc.

When using a garden blower, you're holding it for some time, sort of panning back and forth, with a chainsaw, you're on the side of the tree at the very top if you're a topper (the logger who chops off the top part of the tree) with spikes to hold yourself to the tree with a strap around your waist, or there's the soldier who has two or three point slings so that a weapon/fully automatic weapon can be pivoted in a split second and be ready for a firefight. All of the attributes of these tools serve a purpose for function.

We are just at the start of the action evolution… but this should hopefully start your wheels spinning.

Injuries
(Skip if you are injury-free or under 40)

This is kind of a taboo subject in the business, because no one wants that liability or potential liability, but the truth of the matter is that injuries exist. For a lot of camera operators, it's lower back and shoulders. Stunt people... take your pick.

When I first started becoming involved with stunts, I asked quite a few people how often they worked out and what they did. I was a little surprised, as rarely did any of them work out more than three times a week. However, this may be a nomenclature thing, as a lot of them still practiced falls, fighting, riding dirt bikes, whatever, which they may have considered "staying active," but not "working out."

With operators, I've never asked. However, most operators/DPs I know are a little on the husky side, especially the veterans. Back in the day, cameras were bulky and heavy, and operators certainly beefed up because of it.

Truthfully, in a town like Los Angeles, just like politics, diets and exercise are a religion, and people have opinions about them. What I will offer are some opinions, ideas for various situations.

I remember talking to Dan Kneece, one of the best Steadicam operators around, about his "thing." It was yoga. Yoga is a great foundational step, but like any other practice, done to excess, it will create problems. Also an untrained instructor can set you up for injury. Different fitness studios, for example Yogaworks versus L.A. Fitness, have very different standards for their instructors. L.A. Fitness, for example, has a 200-hour minimum requirement to be able to teach.

Yogaworks requires 500 hours. There's a huge difference between the two.

There are different types of yoga: hatha, hot/Bikram, yin, Iyengar, Kundalini, and each have different influences and results. If you have injuries, yin yoga and restorative yoga are a great route.

Chiropractors or massage therapists are also a good resource, as they can certainly relieve some ailments or stress and injuries almost immediately. Of course, there are different types of chiros, but the truth of the matter is that chiropractic technology 100 years ago was different from what it is now. People would do the service for about a week straight. Now, you may go once a month or week or not at all. It's not everyone's cup of tea. Chiros, to some degree, are, in some circles, still the redheaded stepchild.

Massages are another animal, and they certainly feel good as they can relieve a lot of knots. This too is preventive maintenance. They vary in styles as well, from deep tissue to Swedish. There are also the alternative "massages," like Rolfing, which makes deep tissue feel like a walk in the park, or ART (active release technique), which is a type of myofascial massage, and yes, there will be grimacing with this technique as well. ART massages scar tissue areas, creating flexibility and range in areas that injuries, whether known or not, have locked up.

Another popular form of isolated therapy, a remedy that athletes use to prolong their career or to accelerate their progress, is prolotherapy. Prolotherapy consists basically of injections of a solution of dextrose (sugar) and water. They inject the solution into an injured area and this can *instantly* improve it. Then there is PRP (platelet red plasma), where they extract some blood, put it in a fancy medical "blender" that takes the red cells out, and then put the remaining liquid back into the injured area. More than likely, do prolotherapy first, then PRP. Essentially, prolotherapy is the wholesale solution and PRP is sort of a refinement.* Kobe Bryant made this famous awhile back.

Cortisone was a staple for the longest time, but has long-term detrimental effects.

Now, what do you do if you are on location and hurt yourself?

Obviously diet and staying flexible are critical for preventative maintenance, but sometimes having that camera sitting on your shoulder for hours/days on end can lead to problems.

Egoscue exercise is another option that can be done with a book by following simple directions. Famed football player Junior Seau claimed this gave him his long career.

If you are over 40, as Marcus Allen and Jerry Rice professed, you have to lose weight to take stress off your joints while maintaining speed. Essentially, the body becomes deficient in certain areas, and in some cases, synergistically, this affects the body more. Vitamins and a balanced diet help a lot, and consistent rest will go a long way to optimize body conditions.

There are many schools of thought in this area. Some may treat the doctor's word as gold, and in some cases that really is a must. A doctor is certainly the first person you see if something goes bad.

Mineral balancing is something that is up and coming. The belief is that if the body is lacking in one area, the

---

* http://www.prolotherapy.com

body compensates for it. "Balancing" it can remedy a few situations that you weren't even aware of.

I'm not preaching anything here, just pointing out some options for you that may lead you to a path to help resolve physical problems or encourage preventative maintenance. Either way, awareness is key.

Part 2
Creativity

Creativity

Creativity is something we *all* have innately. How you go about creating is what varies from person to person.

A good friend changed my outlook in terms of putting creativity out there when he explained that he wasn't worried about someone stealing his ideas. He could just create more... There will be people who will tell you to protect your ideas, and in some cases, you should at least be smart about it. Attorneys can certainly put the fear of God into you, and if you are at a Hollywood socialite party, it would be wise to not get drunk or tipsy and blabber off, but the truth of the matter is, creative types will rarely find themselves in those situations, as they are too busy creating rather than schmoozing.

YOU have an unlimited ability to create.

There are always people who you can hang with who would be more than happy to create or collaborate with you. Ultimately, you will find shortly that you'll know whether they are creative or just good at talking.

Creativity can come about in many different forms: daydreaming, being trained classically in an art form, having influential/creative people in your life whether as a young person or as an accomplished professional.

In the 1960s, music went through a major evolution, and drugs were a big part of it. Up until the mid-60s bands sort of had this "look." If you can remember or visualize it, they would all be dressed in suits and had bowl-like haircuts. Then drugs came onto the scene, and everything changed.

I recall an album cover with Ted Nugent, it was still black and white, they had the suits and that bowl cut, and there was Ted with his long hair, a total break with tradition.

The Beatles and The Rolling Stones grew their hair long later, but at the start, they were all somewhat clean-cut. Their music changed dramatically with their look: it went from happy to psychedelic in a matter of a few years, and it became more visceral. Jimi Hendrix had experimented heavily with LSD, Jim Morrison with other drugs, Janis Joplin with the bottle. Each of their last albums were legendary: Hendrix finally got to create the music he wanted with *Band of Gypsies*, Jim Morrison and the Doors with *Soft Parade* and Janis Joplin with *Pearl*. They all paid the price for Art. Each of their creations were revered as masterpieces, but none of them were around to enjoy it.

The truth of the matter is that you don't need external stimulants to have the ability to create.

Then there is the acting world, where the "method" was the staple for many years. Using your own past experiences to create something, made famous by Lee Strasberg, Stanislavski, etc. Eventually, Stella Adler got us away from that.

I can recall seeing Daniel Day Lewis in *Gangs of New York*, where he was masterful. It was personally upsetting when he didn't win the Oscar, as I hadn't seen a performance like that in years. Robert Duvall would always say the character "starts with a walk and a talk," and Lewis's performance epitomized that. Similarly, Heath Ledger in *The Dark Knight* made his character deep, layered and extremely interesting. He was absolutely riveting. Lewis, when he won the

Oscar for *There Will be Blood*, being the classy guy that he is, dedicated his Oscar to Heath.

Another testament to pure visceral acting is Gary Oldman's performance in *The Professional.* That character/performance was unleashed and should be on everyone's viewing list. His work on *Dracula* and *JFK* are memorable as well. It was nice to see Mr. Oldman acknowledged at the 2018 Oscars for his incredible work as Winston Churchill in *Darkest Hour.* Bravo.

I have strong opinions about drugs and filmmaking. If the user is in front of the camera it tends to be interesting, but if the user is behind the camera, it tends to be a bit incoherent.

Nicholson in pretty much anything, but particularly in *Easy Rider*, which was regarded as an avant-garde film; and it should be watched, but it is shocking in terms of the images. Conversely, a movie about drug use, a fine example of what drugs do to the mind and shot appropriately to convey that experience: *Fear and Loathing.*

What inspires you? What floats your boat? What leaves a lasting memory? Is it a movie, a book, location/scenery, a beautiful woman?

I can recall things that grabbed my attention at a very early age, and some of those were not my doing. Some came from my mother playing records of Caruso (one of the opera greats), flamenco and bolero music, Edith Piaf; and my father watching the *Nutcracker* EVERY f**ken year. I was raised in a very blue-collar, middle-class environment where cars and hockey were kings. As time went on, these things germinated in me while I also had my own North-Americanized experiences. Being an only child and living out in the country will certainly make you creative, as there weren't the "luxuries" of such and keeping you indoors. If it was sunny out, and it didn't matter if it was -20 Celsius, there was no argument for staying indoors. The answer was always "out." My father was a man of very few words…

I can recall a comedian talking about being a single parent and not wanting to come down on his kid. Apparently, the kid was bored, but had television, Internet, a PlayStation, and more. The comedian said, when he was young, all he had was a stick. I can relate.

People are losing their viewpoints and their ability to create.

I can recall a survey done in the 1960s, where the average person would experience over 500 pieces of advertising *per day*. Television was in its infancy, radio was fading away, and that was in the *early* 1960s, folks. Move forward 60 years, and now we have smart phones, the Internet, social media. Now the numbers are in the order of 3,800 to 4,200 pieces of advertising per day! I mean, for Pete's sake, there is advertising in urinals! There is no escape. Almost every waking moment, somebody is throwing something in your face.

That has a lot more impact than you might think. *Somebody is telling you what to think!*

It used to be just your parents and relatives, friends and colleagues, and in some cases it was also unfortunately incessant, but it certainly wouldn't be the volume you get from modern-day consumerism. As you get out of the big city and its influences, and into nature, you are getting more control of your own surroundings. I highly recommend it. By having this "luxury," it's possible to have more of your viewpoint.

And viewpoint is king. You, as an artist, have to have your own.

A good friend of mine, Eric Sherman, says "to prepare as a producer or director, a person should work for six months in an insane asylum, six months in a prison for hardcore criminals, and six months in a home for messed-up kids. If you're still on your feet, you may make it in our business!"

I always thought that was a great idea in the sense that you would get an idea of what makes people tick.

For me, for the young guys... I would say hitchhike across the country or up to Alaska, pick a fight with a bigger guy (bruises go away after a few days, but pride will last a lifetime), backpack around India, or on a lighter note ask out the hottest person you see, go for a hike without water, etc. And for God's sake, leave your smart phone at home!

Hell, if that is too much "risk"... start with ordering your Starbucks with regular milk. Trust me... you'll live!

By experiencing life, problems, discoveries... you will start developing your *own* ideas, because the powers that be will do everything possible to take that away from you, and until you have certainty of it, you'll have to figure it out!

Then there are the brokers of chaos[*] working you over pretty good 24/7, 365 days a year. Education can

---

[*] Newspapers, harbingers of evil tidings (news).

also put a damper on your ability to create, due to the standard curriculum, or lack thereof, in most current schools.

A great read is *Dumbing Us Down* by John Taylor Gatto. It will most certainly reveal some paradigms that you might not have been aware of. If you can't be bothered, Ken Robinson has a great TED talk on creativity and how education has curbed it. John and Ken are a teacher and a professor, respectively.

(http://www.ted.com/talks/ken_robinson_says_schools_kill_creativity.html).

A lot happens in our formative years, in terms of flourishing with an unlimited potential to create, or the opposite, where insidious conformity ensues.

There are plenty of books on the subject of imagination. Explore...

Imagination

"A man who has no imagination has no wings."
Muhammad Ali

This can come in many forms, and I'm sure it's an endless stream, hopefully, because without it, we become dead to some extent.

A term that is used in the business/creative world is brainstorming. Is it really "brainstorming?" Not really, but symbolically, I suppose there is some truth to that.

In the kid world, daydreaming would be the more appropriate term, and many of us have been guilty of it. It's not necessarily something we should be "guilty" of in the first place. Essentially, you are bringing to fruition something that came from the mind by way of germinating, refining and evolving.

Allow me to let you in on a secret: you don't need an education to create. This is something that is innate, and we all have it whether we like it or not! That's the good part.

Move forward twenty or thirty or forty years, and where did that daydreaming go? Was it "lost" to our parents telling us to stop daydreaming? In some cases, probably. But the good news is that you can rehabilitate it! I'm sure that there are plenty of methods, and frankly, none are wrong if they stir up the soul, especially, if it's in the area of arts and imagination.

One technique that I use is the idea of combining things that may not necessarily combine in the first place.

For example, I have a particular project that I'm currently working on, a flamenco piece, using stunt principles and 1980s rock concert lighting. If you break it down: why flamenco dancing, why not a different type of dancing? What about stunt principles... what does that even mean? 1980s rock concert lighting? As opposed to 1970s or 1990s rock concert lighting?

The truth of the matter is it's what *I* decided to create.

Somebody else may have a different idea or combination. Maybe, European lighting? The lighting or look is different from North American lighting. You could use film-noir lighting; or maybe instead of "stunt principles" you could use another type of movement. Nothing would be wrong... it's only up to *you* as the creator.

Suppose you have an idea to shoot a scene. Let's say of a woman – mother, wife, girlfriend, sister, pregnant client, etc. They may have some ideas; you may have some of your own. What could *you* combine with *those* ideas? Maybe you need to check out some YouTube videos? Maybe you can pocket some of those ideas until something strikes your fancy and may work together?

Essentially, I have a multitude of ideas. Some are in the back of my mind waiting to be used. Sometimes it's a collaborative effort with other industry professionals.

There need to be some rules when "collaborating." There are *no* wrong ideas, and someone making a snide comment or what have you, does *not* help with the creative process. It actually curbs ideas, whether you are aware of it or not. If you allow the ideas to come without forcing them, even if one idea doesn't match well with that given moment, it may start into something else in the near future. Moreover, when you start creating on another idea, the new idea may combine very well with an old idea.

Get the idea?

A great example of this is in improvisation. In Improv 101, the terms "no" and "but" are taboo. It is always "yes, *and.*" Essentially, somebody is creating an idea, and it leads to another idea, and if another practitioner puts the kibosh on it, that kills it almost instantaneously! Collaborating is no different.

There's a great video of John Cleese (one of the creators behind the Monty Python movies/skits) talking about creativity, and how he creates things versus how his colleagues do it. It's worth a watch: https://www.youtube.com/watch?v=Pb5oIIPO62g.

Note: There's a chance that this link will be inactive in the future, but type in John Cleese, creativity in YouTube… and something will surely come up.

As I mentioned, there are plenty of resources for inspiring yourself. The truth of the matter is, to some degree it's all free, which may or may not need to be said, but I said it.

Sergio Leone's and Ennio Morricone's spaghetti westerns changed how movies were made because of their interesting shots and some truly awesome sound design and music.

Music and sound design can also be used in the combining process.

Even just combining words or nomenclatures can evoke new ideas, because the truth of the matter is, ideas are some of the most powerful concepts known to man. Think communism. What did that word do to the American public during the Cold War? People in the early 1960s, especially during the Bay of Pigs invasion of Cuba, lived in fear.

On a lighter note, I can recall some great lines in Hollywood history. Mr. Eastwood seems to have cornered the market on those. One of the most iconic movie quotes is "go ahead, make my day." If you've never seen *Dirty Harry*, basically the bad guy is holding a gun on Clint's eponymous character. And then Clint points his cannon (Magnum 44) and responds with that line. What he's saying is that he has no fear, so make your move, but it's the *idea* behind the words that has the power.

Another great line is "I love the smell of napalm in the morning." Napalm was a chemical weapon used during the war in Vietnam, and it had a very distinct smell. The writers could've said, I love the smell of the ocean, a campfire, whatever, but again, napalm evoked such an impression, and when the line came from the mouth of a hardass character (played by Robert Duvall), it became an everlasting movie moment.

The filmmaker's or director's interpretation may not always play out, but what I'm trying to convey here is that it's in the *words and the ideas behind them.* Unfortunately, we don't use telepathy, but if we did, words would be rendered useless. Until then, they are used *to convey ideas.*

From my own experience: when I started out, I would call myself a cameraman, camera operator, shooter. However, I literally have been scolded for using the term "shooter." It's a slang term, and in lax environments it would be fine. As things evolved in terms of my shooting style, I started calling myself an "extreme shooter," but, as I mentioned in an earlier chapter, what came about was I was thought of as a dude who liked to shoot with GoPros. This then evolved to a "high-risk shooter," and certainly evoked the greatest responses, bar none. People would just come out and say "what the f**k is that?" Or they would get the idea of helicopters, motorcycles, conflict shooting, etc. Unfortunately, this did have some bad connotations. On one occasion, someone asked me to plant stones, with cameras in them, in the opium line in Afghanistan. Now, years later, I refer to myself as an "action director," because I wear multiple hats, and it encompasses other fields and disciplines that relate to action. When a stunt coordinator says something… I can usually finish the sentence and vice versa. It's a beautiful thing.

Even though words are the vehicle, the ideas themselves are more important. Meaning, *the ideas* will have more impact overall than the words themselves.

One of my favorite stunts of all time was in *Terminator 2*, when Arnold is riding his Harley, cocking his Winchester rifle *while* he is riding. That had been done with horses, and the idea was that in the Old West, when you were being chased or doing the chasing, you had to reload quickly to "respond."

It was James Cameron's ingenious idea of combining that with a Harley. It's not the hardest stunt, or mind-blowing by any means, but it did leave an impression on me. And trust me, having the biggest budget in the world doesn't necessarily mean you'll have the biggest return in the world.

Look what *Star Wars* did to the sci-fi genre. It changed everything. It set a new bar.

Music in the early nineties took a bit of a different twist. I can recall Lenny Kravitz using music equipment from the 1960s and 1970s, as he wanted to give his music a bit of a different sound. A little more raw or unrefined, if you will. Even with professional post-sound software, you can use a 1960s-1970s Marshall amp to give it that not-so-polished sound.

The Rolling Stones in their prime, in my opinion, the 1969-1974 Mick Taylor era, created some sounds and used instruments that made for timeless songs. Led Zeppelin was making music history at the time as well. Note: Led Zeppelin never had a #1 hit in the States.

It's an era of music making that was truly, revolutionary and trailblazing.

You can't consider music and imagination without considering David Bowie and The Beatles. They each did something very unusual and unique. The Beatles created *Sgt. Pepper's Lonely Hearts Club Band* and allowed *the characters* to create the music, *not the musicians themselves*. David Bowie did the same with *Ziggy Stardust*. They both created *characters*. The characters lived through them, and they allowed them feel and to create, accordingly.

To this day, David Bowie is still considered to have had the most influence on the bands of the last thirty years of all the musicians of our generation. He will be missed.

The combinations are endless, and your ability to create ideas is also endless. You, the artist, are responsible for impressing minds, and hopefully for the better.

Below is great exercise for creating new ideas.

This is a very simple technique, which is one of the things that makes it so effective. It is also a great introduction to creativity. It brings two things together that do not ordinarily connect in our minds or in the real world. It does this in a setting where we are open and receptive to making connections, and it does it in a way that is random and likely to stimulate new ideas.

This can be used by an individual or in small groups of two to four people. You will need a stack of 3x5 cards or several pieces of paper and a pen.

Start by writing down any ideas that you have on the cards. Each idea is written on a separate card. What you write on the card should be descriptive. Not just "basketball player," but more like "a basketball player aggressively dribbling down the court." Instead of "a birthday cake," it should be "a chocolate birthday cake with vanilla frosting and candles." Instead of "a dog," perhaps "a white shaggy dog in a woman's purse." You get the idea. Just be very descriptive.

Write down a bunch of ideas, each one on its own card. Then, turn all of the cards face down and shuffle them so they are in no particular order.

With the cards facing down so that you can't tell what is on them, select two cards at random and turn them face up so that you can read what is on them.

Each of the ideas on the cards has something to do with the objective. As you randomly turn them over in pairs, they bring ideas together that you may not have thought to connect. Your exercise is to try and make the ideas on the cards connect in some way, which can stimulate new ideas.

I once saw, during a workshop, a painter and a photographer team up to use this technique. The photographer's objective was to create a dynamic image for his portfolio. He primarily photographed sports and wanted to create a dynamic image of action. The two came up with quite a few ideas that were written down on 3x5 cards. These were phrases that described action, energy and sports. One of the sets of cards they turned over was: "a basketball player aggressively dribbling down the court" and "a Tesla coil lamp with lightning bolts" (this is a large glass globe with electricity arcing inside the globe). These two cards sparked the image of a basketball player slam-dunking the ball. He is mid-air, and he is so energized that energy is arcing from him as he leaps. A dynamic image for sure.

When you have paired up all of the cards, you can end the exercise, or you can reshuffle the cards and do it again. You could also write more ideas on cards and then reshuffle all the cards and do it again. Who knows what could come out of this…

Sometimes people believe they need to have some sort of "inspiration." Drugs, a log cabin in the woods of Alaska, a muse, etc.

A friend of mine in the past was deep into secret societies and travelled to Paris to go to one of the original Freemason lodges, Grand Orient de France (this was a particular group in the world of Freemasonry, to keep things simple).

Next door was a famous bar where you could imbibe absinthe. Paris was the place where it was happening, and many famous people drank it: Ernest Hemingway, Vincent Van Gogh, Oscar Wilde, Aleister Crowley, etc. In fact, one of my favorite artists, Edgar Degas, depicted the look of an Absinthe drinker in one of his pieces. Absinthe was eventually banned in the U.S. for having psychotropic qualities.

Anyhow, my friend went to the bar next door to the Grand Lodge in Paris and ordered a drink of absinthe. A beautiful woman accompanied him during his consumption of the drink(s). He thought this was odd but wasn't complaining.

When he decided to pay the bill, it came out to 500 euros, which at the time was equivalent to $750. The response of my friend, to say the least, was "WTF? I just ordered two drinks!" The response was something to this effect of, "well sir, the drinks were so and so price, but the beautiful lady was your muse, and hopefully she inspired you?"

You see, these famous artists and poets would go in there to get "inspired," but truthfully that was just a cop- out. Certainly, a beautiful woman has qualities that can make the toughest of men act like (fill answer here) _____, and they also have other qualities, which have been responsible for some great pieces of art. Unfortunately, this bar burned down a couple of years ago.

Jimi Hendrix was someone else who experimented heavily with psychedelics/acid and paid the price. A friend of mine used to frequent his place when he was in Sausilito, and he said that the place was always "filled" with blondes. Maybe it wasn't all the partying that killed him…

Probably one of the most notables of imagination would be Leonardo da Vinci. The original Renaissance Man. Da Vinci was well-versed in classical arts, but was an inventor, mathematician, engineer and probably a few other things. In addition to being an artist worthy of note and painting the Mona Lisa, he had original ideas for a helicopter, a tank, solar power, etc. and that was 500 years ago! His ability to create things was off the charts. He not only didn't have anything to relate to as things were not mass-produced yet, as the industrial revolution wouldn't happen for another 300-400 years, but he was able to conceptualize his ideas.

Spending a lot of time in Italy, I could see some of Da Vinci's influences. There's a particular bird which influenced how he came up with the idea of a plane. That's all he had to work with conceptually.

The point I'm making here was that he was able to take ideas from other areas and fields and make them work.

You as an artist are able to do the same... just create.

Perceptions

It's been a long-standing tradition, which was agreed by certain groups, even cabals, that we have five senses: sight, hearing, smell, taste and touch.

This has been promoted primarily and heavily by psychiatry and psychology.

In the heyday, producers and directors in the 1930s and 1940s went to Germany to study the "mind." Sigmund Freud was in demand in Hollywood. He had even been approached to write a script... despite being a man who believed that actors were crazy! Sure, I've met a couple of those, but the whole lot, Mr. Freud? "Professor" Wundt didn't help the situation either as he believe man was an animal without a soul.

Having someone gauge a person clinically in a field where aesthetics are senior to his limited approach seems absurd to me.

Let's take a look at wavelengths. Have you ever met a calming person? How about someone having a bad day? Or even worse, a cop having a bad day! How about a sunny day when all is well? What about a movie or book that leaves you with this ecstatic feeling? These experiences are things you *perceive* not with the five senses, just the apparency of them. The five sense have been agreed upon so many years ago, they are no longer challenged in this modern day.

A blind man whose hearing is so developed that his eye muscles become relaxed starts getting crazy eyes, and what occurs is the reduction of other senses while one develops more.

During my application process to work on a search and rescue team in the mountains of British Columbia, I had an interesting experience. Part of the application was a gauge of my familiarity with each mountain. For example, how many times have you climbed each one and at what times of year? This made a difference because of variations such as in the spring, the foliage was greater and you couldn't see as much as in the winter when the leaves would fall away. Also, foliage was dictated by elevation. In winter, the snow would cover certain rocks. Or the sun's placement during the year could create shadows and "hide" things. And this was for trails, never mind the gulches (very narrow valleys).

I was quite familiar with the mountains, to the point where for most of these areas, I would use a loop trail that would lead to another trail, because coming down the same way that you go up is boring. It's not like Los Angeles where you can see the view as you are ascending. In the Pacific Northwest/British Columbia you have only vista points, and in some cases only at the top, which can be a very rewarding experience. For a week, I monitored the sunset and knew to the minute when the sunlight was no more.

For this particular hike, it turns out there was not a different descending trail that I could find. I had never used a book, and the Internet was in its infancy for these types of things back then. I spent extra time looking for the trail, which was now cutting into my time to get back. And what I had not considered was the height of the trees. This created a problem. I was now late and started to run down to the point where I couldn't see the fluorescent ribbons (up there they use ribbons, whereas in the States, they use a metal arrow with reflective paint). Lo and behold, I could not see anymore. Yeah… fuck.

I could hear a stream not too far away and worked towards it. With this, there was an opening in the forest, and every so often the moon would shine through, so at least I could see where I was walking. I went on for hours. Every so often, I couldn't move forward and would have to go around by way of going up the embankment and cutting back in; if I were lucky without eating some dirt, literally. One problem, I knew, was that creeks don't always go down straight and essentially could bring me around the mountain.

Now, at this *very* moment, after doing this for some time, I heard a different noise, because my hearing sense had developed in a very short time. I stood still and listened. I could always hear the water trickling by, but this was different.

I looked down and realized that I was standing on the edge of a cliff. The sound that had changed was the water descending and hitting the fallen trees. Moreover, both of my feet were about a third over the edge. One more step and the crows would have been picking out my eyeballs!

The best part was getting down from there. I had to descend a mossy cliff, roughly sixty feet, in the dark, with the water trickling over me. Fun stuff.

Because I couldn't see where my hands and feet were, I had to feel my way to make sure it was secure with each movement. My tactile perception was now enhanced – big time. After another couple of hours, I had made it down. I've had other risky situations worse than that, but I used this example to illustrate what happened when I lost light and had to rely on other senses.

Which brings me to my next example: Beethoven. How did he compose after the loss of his hearing? In one person's assessment, it was his "mind's ear." Interesting. Could it be that he could see the imagery of his notes? This would be my strongest conjecture.

I know personally when I am in tune with music, I actually see and perceive the musician as if they are right in front of me. This has developed over time. I used to think I was lyrically deaf for a long time, as I didn't hear the lyrics but could hear *every* little musical idiosyncrasy. I'm not formally trained in music, so my scope of nomenclature is limited.

Can you recall a time when you were hit on? Did your "antennas" perk up? What were they picking up? Is it a "sense," is it "vibe," or as Southern Californians say... your "energy"?

When looking at body language, you are essentially looking at what's going on in people's lives by way of body manifestations.

Is the person walking in an extroverted manner? Like they are on a stroll at a park or museum? How about somebody at a riot or protest? Are their movements graceful or deliberate? How about a street dog that is skittish? How many times do you think that animal was kicked or abused?

Your observations of the above examples are a reflection of your awareness, which has nothing to do with your five senses. For example, in the dog's case, it is scared of being kicked/hurt, so it is jumpy. What are you truly observing there?

How many times have you been speeding on a highway and you just decided to slow down, and sure enough there was a cop down the road or around the corner?

A couple of weeks ago I was at an office I frequent. The admin went for the phone *before* it even rang. It was a fraction of a second difference, but nevertheless she perceived it was going to ring. How did she do it? I have my opinions on it.

Science doesn't allow you to perceive, because it can't be measured. Does that mean it doesn't exist?

It is one of these reasons why we, in Hollywood, have lost our way. We now use algorithms to create success, or we have MBAs who tell calculate spending X number of dollars to equate to Y number of potential audience members coming to the theater.

How exactly did that work with the *Blair Witch Project, Beasts of the Southern Wild* or *City of God*? What about action movies like the original *Mad Max* and *Bloodsport*?

Action movies generally cost more, because there is danger involved by way of the stunts, but you don't always have to spend the bucks for the talent.

With *Crank* (Jason Statham was already a star), it was made for $12 million. Jason is the exception to the rule and works extremely hard at his craft. Not everyone can do their own stunts, but he, like Stallone before him, put the extra mile in.

I believe the *Bond* movies had a $30 million budget *just* for the stunts, and that was the standard... and then a successful little series came along, *Bourne*, and changed the genre.

Follow my insight, and you'll have more bang for your buck in shooting action.

Movements

Movements are an integral part of action or second unit, because you need to sell it. You can't phone in a fight sequence, the audience will know. The stunt driver has to over-embellish the loss of control of the car or that it's hard to handle. With motorcycles this is the contrary; and as a result makes it look to easy when it really isn't!

Wrong or right, the camera doesn't lie! Whatever you communicate by way of movement *will* be noticed.

The thing with actors versus stunt people is that actors are showing their emotions via close ups and being lit properly, etc. Stunt professionals are selling it physically.

Most people can do one or the other but rarely both. Douglas Fairbanks, John Wayne, Richard Burton, Sylvester Stallone, Tom Cruise, Jason Statham and some others were/are able to do both. Essentially you are doing two different things, but it ends up in the same place: the camera.

Different movements create different effects. Watching Baryshnikov (ballet), Bobby Orr (hockey) or Michael Jordan (basketball) in their heyday was seeing beauty in motion. They all served a purpose for what they were doing, but only Baryshnikov was selling it to the audience, while Orr and Jordan were doing it for points or wins.

Interestingly enough, it was generally understood that Orr was a scoring machine, but it was his skating ability that was the catalyst. In other words, his ability to move his legs gave him the edge. Orr changed the game.

Wayne Gretzky's father didn't allow Wayne to use a hockey stick until he was a proficient skater, and that worked out pretty well for him too.

Then there are the Whirling Dervish[*] of the Sufi Order who employ their dance for religious purposes (worship, prayer, meditation, etc.). It's quite a sight to be seen! In some cases, they are spinning for quite a few minutes.

To take this even further, my good friend Anthony De Longis, a master of the blade and movements, shared this with me:

"One of the keys to success with the whip (and virtually any other sport or martial art) is that all the parts of the body, and by extension, the whip, are doing the same thing at the same time and *nothing more*. This is where most people are inefficient or downright hazardous to themselves and everyone around them.

There are eight angles of attack in all martial- and bladed-weapons systems, including the empty-hands arts. I consider the whip a super-sonic telescoping blade (it shatters the sound barrier at over 768 mph/1400 fps). The unique 'De Longis Rolling Loop' methodology I created is more efficient/effective/accurate and combative – the tip of the whip stabbing at the instant of impact instead of just slashing. It can be delivered to any of the eight attacking angles with great speed and precision by an adjustment of the hand that instantly changes the angle of the strike, and by a simple manipulation of the wrist I can even strike around corners to hit my selected target from behind."

---

[*] http://en.wikipedia.org/wiki/Sufi_whirling

The two things that really hit home for me in this piece of wisdom, were an "adjustment of the hand" and "a simple manipulation of the wrist." These two actions are the difference between mastery and real-world circumstances of a life-or-death situation. Good stuff!

Roughly a century ago there was a fellow who was present at a volcano while it was erupting. That is where the Parkour technique was born. Under duress and panic, people generally don't worry about technique. It's the school of "get the hell out of here!" Many years later, it was used in an elite firefighting unit in France. The father passed it down to his son, David Belle. David is the guy who put Parkour/freerunning on the map. If you are not familiar with Parkour or David Belle, I recommend watching *District B-13*.

These movements developed over time and combined with other movements have evolved into other creations. For example, a Parkour/freerunning guy with a background in martial arts will have some different moves. Mind you, there are codified moves that can be discussed anywhere on the planet in relation to cinematic moves, L.A., Paris or even Hong Kong. This chapter isn't about Parkour, but it gives an idea how movements have developed.

One of the reasons Baryshnikov was a household name when he came to the United States was because that was pure ballet. Over the last 30 years, the balletic art has been altered, even bastardized, if you will.

Russia in Baryshnikov's time was dominant in so many fields: gymnastics, hockey, ballet. Their work ethic and skills were on another level. A lot of these athletes and dancers, after their amateur careers, came to Hollywood and they already had the discipline to become a stunt person. Obviously, there are other aspects of stunts that are done by other stunt people, high falls (divers), fight sequences (ex-fighters), etc.

In Los Angeles, Santa Monica, specifically at the Pier, just north of it, you will find on Sundays various artists practicing their art/discipline. You'll see gymnastics, tight-rope walking, cheerleading, capoeira, rings, all involving people using their own body weight to do various actions. Santa Monica is home to the original Muscle Beach. Each one of those actions tells a story.

Here's the thing, and it's important. Instead of using talent as talent, use it as a tool in the creative process.

For the record, in production, the equipment we use is referred to as "tools." Anything from a Panasonic GH5 or Sony A7S for budgetary purposes to an Arri or RED when you have the monetary support to create and maximize the image, all of these are "tools." However, I do like the word "instrument" as opposed to tool. "Tool" has a carpentry/trade connotation attached to it, whereas an "instrument" conjures this idea of an orchestra where all of the instruments are in sync. Moreover, talented individuals work extremely hard on what they do, even though, in some cases, they are treated like second-class citizens.

These "instruments" can be used to create a motion that is pleasing to the eye *and* can forward the story. In other words, they use the camera.

You need a Parkour athlete to create a *specific* motion, or a drifting car to create another, as an example.

Having said that, *you need to know the basics in filmmaking.* For example, when panning, there's a certain speed at which you can pan. With a longer length, that's more amplified. Another example is the horizon[*] of the camera.

Another movement that has become common here in the last decade, but originated in Hong Kong, is wires for pulling actors, stunt people or what have you. It's a natural motion that is more calming to the eye, whereas CGI can be an unnatural movement, especially in the field of physics, but are pretty damn close!

There are many different types of movements you can incorporate into a shot…

An ultimate/Russian arm, technocrane, crane, jib or slider all serve a purpose and have a certain look and feel, but this is *still* based on movement, some potentially fast and some slow. Moreover, the eyes and brain and how we perceive are additional factors that have to be considered.

For the same reason, when Hollywood was doing 3D in post-production versus in production, there were things being worked out. Generally, people who were over of the age of 40 complained, more so if they wore glasses. Whereas gamers[†] were not affected.

To further this point, as I mentioned earlier, the zoom has an unnatural feeling to the eye. However, a slow zoom in, at a crucial and insightful point, is an art form in itself.

---

[*] Keeping the camera level. If it becomes askew while in motion, it takes the audience out of the moment, breaking the fourth wall.

[†] Gamers are people who play video games regularly.

ALL of the above fall under the category of movement.

You are the artist. Not the manufacturers. **You** *decide what is pleasing to the eye, and it would be wise to know these scientific points.*

Marketing has been so insidious that we've lost some of our ways. This is the reason I want to discuss the difference between a tool and an instrument.

I recall some kids in New Orleans years ago with bottle caps on the bottoms of their shoes tap dancing - quite well I might add. Also there was the fellow using multiple five-gallon pails as a drum set. It was amazing! Neil Pearl would have given him the nod (drummer from Rush).

Buckets, people…

He turned a tool into an instrument.

When you start studying movements, you'll start finding or creating tools to turn into instruments. Hell, you'll be able to go to your favorite camera/stunt store and rig something yourself. We have become a society of "I'll buy a new or better one."

I would do just that. There are plenty of options: a sailing store, Home Depot, my garage, etc. Start fabricating stuff. Even if it doesn't work, you'll know the next time, and you'll understand the mechanics, physics and motions of it. *That* is invaluable, and frankly, a necessary step in the learning process.

I recall having a great chat with an A-lister about just that. I had made a documentary and had done pretty much everything wrong. "That's how you learn," he said. And he was right.

My buddy Garrett did that too. He did a 150-foot fall with a fabricated sling while shooting the camera. Then, he used it in a parachute shoot that he did recently. Special forces I'm sure have similar systems but used in different applications.

What I'm getting you to do is to look at *all* possibilities and combinations for creating that shot.

Note: Getting that shot *versus* getting that shot with the principles of cinematography are two different things.

Mood Lines

There are many basic books for cinematography, with three books being sort of the standard. *The Five C's of Cinematography* by Joseph V. Mascelli, *Cinematography* by Kris Malkiewicz and *Painting with Light* by John Alton (tough read, as a lot of the technology is not current and it's hard to relate to, but it is still considered a standard). You'll find that most classically trained cinematographers have read these books. *How to Shoot a Movie and Video Story* by Arthur Gaskell is a great complement to this list.

The one book I use for reference continually is the *The Five C's of Cinematography*. It's well-written and elaborates the craft insightfully. In all the books on the subject, there is one concept that, as far as I know, was never used in modern filmmaking, but very much is used in the fields of advertising, designers and architecture: mood lines.

Lines can control and orient the eyes and can be more efficient in capturing the viewer's imagination. There are certain principles laid out in *The Five C's of Cinematography*. One of the earliest examples of this was a documentary that was created by the Department of Agriculture. It was beautifully shot and was a classic example of mood lines. It was so well-done, people claim it should've been considered for an Oscar, but because it was a documentary and existed outside the Hollywood system, it wasn't considered.

The movie was used in the USC film program to illustrate the concept of a tone poem (a piece of orchestral music, typically in one movement. There's a poem that is repeatedly said throughout).

The thing about this film, which was shot during the Depression, is that within the framing there were ascending and descending lines. Just like ascending or descending a mountain. The lines represented the time period.

In advertising, it's much more simplistic, but nevertheless can be used on a grander scale. Research has shown that you have to get the viewer's attention in less than a second. The same could be said for websites. How much time will you spend on a site before you move onto something else? We're obviously not talking about advertising or websites, what we are talking about is *creating as much impact as we can in the shortest period of time.*

This technique or method is still used in architecture. Mood lines have been around since the beginning of recorded time, as they are based on geometric shapes, and the land has offered these things to us naturally.

Mood lines are a *very* effective tool for creating more impact with your images. There is a difference between a line and a mood line, in the sense that a line will just control your eye, where the mood line will hold your emotion, hence the name.

The thing about shooting action or action films is that the images are *very* short, so you have to create as much impact as possible. With cinematography, the framing and composition may dictate how that is done depending on budget, skill and location, but mood lines, when intercut with other images, will create an overall sensation.

A great example of this was in *Robin Hood* with Russell Crowe, especially the final battle that took place at the end of the movie. Lots of confusion, lots of blood and guts, but there were some cuts in relation to the other boats that were coming in, that were too static. As a result, it took the believability out of it for me. You sort of lose momentum. FYI, battle scenes are no cakewalk to shoot, as there are a lot of factors that come into play. It just so happens that a couple of images can detract from the whole scene, impact-wise. Obviously, the editing department has to be considered.

Mood lines are a tool used to create more impact to your vision. Remember, you have a fraction of second to create an impression on somebody's mind…

On the next page is a layout of mood lines courtesy of *From Landscape Architecture* by John Ormsbee Simonds & Barry Starke. Published by McGraw-Hill Book Company, Inc.

Active	Passive	Structural Solid Strong	Nonstructural Fluid Soft
Stable	Unstable	Positive Bold Forceful	Tenuous Uncertain Wavering
Primitive Simple Bold	Effusive	Flamboyant	Refined
Rough Rasping Grating	Smooth Swelling Sliding	Decreasing Contracting	Increasing Expanding
In Motion	Meandering Casual Relaxed Interesting Human	Erratic Bumbling Chaotic Confused	Logical Planned Orderly
Rising Optimistic Successful Happy	Falling Pessimistic Defeated Depressed	Indecisive Weak	Rise Fall
Indirect Plodding	Concentrating Assembling	Dispersing Fleeing	Opposing
Connecting Crossing	Parallel Opposing with harmony	Excited Nervous Jittery	Opposing with friction
Stable	Unstable	Flowing Rolling	Formal Priestly Imperious Dogmatic
The Vertical Noble Dramatic Inspirational Aspiring	The Horizontal Earthy Calm Mundane Satisfied	Progressive	Regressive
Jagged Brutal Hard Vigorous Masculine Picturesque	Curvilinear Tender Pleasant Soft Feminine Beautiful	Broken Interrupted Severed	Direct Sure Forceful with Purpose
Dynamic	Static Focal Fixed	Diverging Dividing	Growing Developing

Lighting for Second Unit

Some may say that Caravaggio is the godfather of cinematography, and other notable figures are Rembrandt, Vermeer etc. This is Cinematography 101.

Let's talk about Kelvins (K): the measurement of heat, and the main unit of the cinematographer in terms of temperature color.

Rembrandt, a resident of Northern Europe, had a different kind of light. Vermeer was known for painting using the light coming from windows. Tungsten at 3200K provides warm light, while daylight at 5600K is cooler. These are the two most commonly used temperatures in the business.

However, this book is mainly for action or second unit, and frankly, there are a lot of cinematographers who are much more skilled in this area than I and who could go into much greater detail. What I can provide will at least give you an idea or boundaries to think with.

What I was told, rather than what I have read, is that the two different light colors were born out of blacksmithing. A blacksmith would put iron in the fire and the temperature to which the metal would heat would vary. There is a wide variance in terms of temperatures (colors) from 1700K to 27000K that the metal reaches in the fire.

To make this simple, we will use only 3200K to 5600K. If you want to learn more about this, there are plenty of other resources.

A lot of stunts and action scenes are shot outside. Obviously, with green screen mainly indoors, you'll need to get more education on the subject and use a competent director of photography (DP).

The good stuff, in a nutshell - and there will be lots of arguments regarding this but it doesn't matter - is as follows.

Let's suppose I was to categorize the two different units – first unit (lighting) and action/second unit (movement).

Lighting, the responsibility of the cinematographer/DP, provides mood, orientation, texture: the shaping of light, etc.

Movement, or action, provides culture, texture, locations, etc. I delved into this blindly for almost two years before results came into fruition.

Getting back on track, let's talk about lighting for outdoors.

Storraro (*Apocalypse Now*, *Ladyhawke*) rarely shoots between the hours of 11AM and 4PM because of the placement of the sun, which would be dictated by the latitude of the country and time of year.

Ingmar Bergman is a master of creating texture using natural and simplistic settings for most of his films. His *Seventh Seal* is one of those movies you need to watch for texture. Leaves, trees can be a great tool to shape a scene and give it a certain feel.

Due to my Heli-logging and search and rescue days, I myself know where certain trees are in terms of altitude or the relationship to other things, and as a result, I can take advantage of the seasons (I will talk more about this in "Scouting").

Another movie that is a must-see is *I Am Cuba*, especially for its camera movements. It was ahead of its time on so many levels. I might add that "kitchen utensils" were used in the production.

Martin Scorsese and Francis Ford Coppola were consummate in giving credit where it was due. *I Am Cuba* influenced Coppola in *Apocalypse Now*. More so for the cinematography than the camera movements, which are also stunning.

The three other modern-day cinematographers of note in this arena are Jeff Cronenweth (*The Girl with the Dragon Tattoo, The Social Network*), Caleb Deschanel (*The Patriot, The Passion of the Christ*) and Conrad Hall (*Road to Perdition, American Beauty*), whom I will talk about, but there are plenty of other amazing cinematographers like Roger Deakins (*Skyfall, Shawshank Redemption*), the Coen Brothers (most of their films), Wally Pfister (*Batman, Memento* and *Inception*), Vilmos Zsigmond (*Deliverance, The Deer Hunter, Close Encounters of the Third Kind*) and Christopher Doyle (*Hero, In the Mood for Love*).

The great thing about movies is that you can get lost in the beauty of the things that they create. In most cases, it's a matter of a few seconds, and it is my initial reaction to the aforementioned DPs, Croneweth, Deschanel and Conrad Hall, with regard to watching their work.

My mentor and dear friend, Howard Wexler, called me from Hawaii one day and suggested that I watch *The Girl with the Dragon Tattoo*, as it had a great chase sequence. A month or two later, I was able to hear Jeff Croneweth speak at a convention where he showed us three scenes and talked about each one; and one of the scenes was that chase sequence. When the opening scene came on, I felt like a little kid again, I was lost in the magic of the movie. You see, the opening sequence takes place in Sweden, and the mood, the look and pace were almost identical to the area I was raised in Canada. Then there was this chase sequence... Jeff described how he did it: he created the illusion of speed by way of strobing, notably in a first-unit fashion; and this has become a standard for me on how to imbue beauty into a stunt. An action guy will look at the scene another way. There is no right way, and I will go over different perspectives depending on backgrounds, whether stunts, VFX or cinematography to show the contrast.

The scenes moved me so much that I was obsessed with seeing *The Girl with the Dragon Tattoo*. I drove home to find out where I could find it in a theater, as it hadn't come out on DVD yet. I think I drove from Manhattan Beach out to some place in Corona where I found one of those three-dollar theatres where the bulb in the projector was worn out probably three years ago, and had people talking throughout the movie. No fun.

Even with the disappointment of the crummy theater I thought to myself "how did some guy from Malibu know how to create scenes like that?"

At a party a several weeks later, Shane Hurlbut was giving a talk on Canon products. I was kind of tired and had just finished a heavy work schedule prior, but Jeff Cronenworth was standing next to me and I thought... what the hell? I introduced myself... and the whole time, I have this burning question "How did you figure out that shot/look in Sweden, especially since you were raised in Malibu?" I'm waiting for this profound answer and hanging on to each word. But, what Jeff said was something to the effect of, "well, when it's 20 Celsius below, you figure it out pretty quick."

Conrad Hall. You won't find too many people in the cinematography community who won't speak with total admiration of Mr. Hall's work. Watch the first 30 seconds of *Road to Perdition* with Tom Hanks. That's all you need to see to know you are watching a master.

There's a common thread among the greats that you'll hear quite often: seamless cinematography. In other words, you don't notice the shots going from one to another. Not too showy, in other words.

From a second-unit perspective, this applies to some degree, but since we are dealing with movement more than lighting, there is generally a flow that has to be captured by the editor (I will talk about this in great detail later in "Editing").

For second unit or action, the pace or rhythm is dictated by the story, and the action is what drives it. A Kubrick movie, which is not seamless by any stretch of the imagination, is still very engaging despite the abruptness. In fact, in *2001: A Space Odyssey* or *A Clockwork Orange*, those abrupt shots/stills add flavor, texture, impact to the movie.

Caleb Deschanel. It was during the opening sequence of *The Patriot* that I realized what cinematography was. I had read about it, studied it, heard about it, but during that sequence, it became very real for me. The first few minutes capture a time of innocence, a time of no worries, with corresponding texture, mood and orientation etc. It's a masterpiece. His work on *The Passion of the Christ* cannot be ignored either.

Standard operating procedure for studying a cinematographer is to shut off the volume on the film so as to not be influenced by sound, dialogue, etc.

As a drill you can, and should, watch both those movies, *The Patriot* and *The Passion of the Christ* with the volume off, or at the very least the opening sequence of *The Patriot*. If you don't know what's going on just based on the images, I would be very surprised.

In closing, look at what the masters have done and have a library of go-to movies for inspiration. All the greats do...

Note: A production/art designer is also a key component for setting the mood or locale.

Scouting

This is one my favorite aspects of the filmmaking process. Choosing the right locations is the part that will give that little bit of flavor to the scene, so to speak.

When scouting, there are many factors. You are trying to maximize the amounts of shots you can take in one place as well as enhance the mood and forward the story, not to mention noticing the movement of the sun that can cause limitations and time constraints.

Is it a car chase with the police chasing the bad guys in an industrial area? Or is it some good ol' boys being chased out in the country? That's two different looks. And because of those different scenarios, you need two different locations.

If you shoot from one direction... can you use the other direction for shooting too? Is the road surface satisfactory? Does it have the feel you're looking for, especially at high speeds? Do the tree shadows give more texture to the road when the sun comes through the trees? Where's the sun? Is the sun at the same place at different times of year, as principal shooting will take place for a few weeks? What about buildings versus trees? The list goes on...

Then there's the city, and something I learned from Vilmos Zsigmond. Vilmos once used six rooms in a hotel to shoot a movie. Each room had been set up for a different scene, so essentially he could go from room to room. I used the same principle for some guerilla shooting. It was in a less affluent neighborhood, close to the water/ports. Essentially, due to the proximity to the ports and the vehicle, I could have six locations in one.

The thing about less affluent neighborhoods is the turnaround times for the police are, truthfullly, much longer. I found in these types of neighborhoods residents usually bring out the camera instead of calling the police. In Beverly Hills, Manhattan Beach, Burbank, etc., the police will be there in three minutes. Would L.A.P.D. do the same? They can't be concerned with these things sometimes.

On one shoot, the car was so loud that every time the driver hit the gas you thought the world was coming to an end! It was pretty awesome, but a liability. I had a shot list with a variance in equipment for creative reasons, so we executed in a proficient manner with the least amount of fuss or detection. I treat this type of shooting group more like a tight military crew, which I will talk more about later. Everyone knew *exactly* what they had to do. You are only good as your weakest link.

If the shoot is a little more radical, safety first and by the book with permits. No exceptions.

The more guerilla or risky the shots, the more times I scout.

I need to know for sure and I can't have any doubt in my mind. None.

When scouting or considering shooting near trains, ports or airports, you have to be vigilant. If you are carrying a camera, in the States, you will be considered a suspicious character. If you get pulled over or stopped by the police in one of these areas three times, you get on a watch list. It would be wise if and when this does happen to be on your best behavior and be, or at least look, as legit as possible.

One time I was shooting a time-lapse of the San Pedro harbor. I was at a high vantage point that overlooked the harbor. I wanted time-lapse of the cranes going up and down and of the big vessels coming in. I actually did notice two police vehicles below. It wasn't more than five minutes before one of the police officers came up to investigate what I was doing. The standard questions, I.D. and so on. He was a good guy, but what he told me is that they had over twenty cameras on me! I'm not sure if that was B.S., but that's enough for me to just to find something or somewhere else. No attitude, ladies and gentlemen.

We are artists and have unlimited abilities to create. It's safer to do it by the book with permits, which is not always easy, unfortunately.

Another scouting scenario:

I had something I wanted to shoot under the Redondo Beach pier, where I wanted to kayak under the columns where the waves came in. I visited the area three different times to look at the waves, dealing with other potential people, what time the coast guard comes in, and lastly to find the best lighting. I walked the area several ways too.

I timed it for the day of the six-man volleyball tournament in Manhattan Beach (annual event – the biggest event of the year in this town). The local police are very concerned about the tournament going bad, and they call in reinforcements from other cities, because of a riot that took place in Huntington Beach in the late 80s. Which meant the coast was actually clear in Redondo Beach. Everyone was in Manhattan Beach, ready for a riot! So, I took advantage of the paranoia.

I get out there and I do an Eskimo roll (where you roll the kayak over 360 degrees). The camera came off my head, and I had to get it back on my head underwater while holding the paddle in the other hand.

I have been kayaking for over twenty years, and my father was an ex-frogman (a precursor to the Navy SEALs), so I had trained since a young boy to be able to hold my breath for several minutes, and I would consider myself an above-average swimmer. Due to the location and shot I didn't have another kayaker close by, because I didn't want him in the shot either.

Shit happens, but I kept my cool because I have trained for this many times with other similar scenarios. That, as far as I'm concerned, is the most important thing – keeping your cool.

You can do things by the book or to your satisfaction, but more importantly, if there are other people's lives at stake, you need to take responsibility for them. *No exceptions.* Depending on the size of the shoot/crew there may not be a producer, so you have to take responsibility for all.

However, gauging talent for action or second unit is a *whole* other world. What someone can tolerate and their skill level has to be determined *beforehand.* Something I found with producers is that they are a little unaware of these factors; and especially directors, as they are good with story, not action. Do your homework!

As your eyes get trained and you work in different locales, speak to veterans and location managers to get a wider scope for variance in terms of looks. There are plenty of places to choose from to give something a particular "look."

On the central coast, there are two unique places, one looks like the Serengeti and another looks like the Deep South with weeping willows.

This is part of movie magic: creating a belief that that is the real location. Sometimes you'll find these locations that look just like somewhere else on the planet.

One time in the Dominican Republic, I came out of this forest/jungle into a village where they were setting up a boar for a feast. They were literally "plunging" the boar to be ready for a spit, which is quite a sight, and in the distance I saw these mountains that looked very similar to the mountains of China (*Man with the Golden Gun*, *The Bourne Legacy* closing shots).

Another time while in Panama I was hanging out with an engineer on the canal, and he claimed that certain hills had gold in them. A few years later, I recall driving up to Kelowna from Vancouver, British Columbia and seeing identical looking hills, and lo and behold there was a sign – historical gold rush site.

You'll have to find substitutions. The ones I've described wouldn't necessarily be cost-effective in terms of travelling expenses, but they were used here for illustrative purposes.

A few years back I saw the movie *The Grey* with some friends. In the movie, there's a plane crash out in the middle of nowhere in the Arctic, if I recall. It's just white (from the snow) when they crash, with no reference points. Obviously, they need to get out of there and have to deal with a wolf chasing them.

So, during their jaunt, the viewer sees a lot of landscapes. I could see that these were not true in the sense of elevations. Mountains look a certain way, or the rocks on the side of the creek, trees at a certain altitude... to me, these all tell a story; which in my professional opinion was not accurate.

Now, my buddies who obviously didn't have the same background and possibly were city folks seemed quite enthralled by it. Sometimes it just doesn't matter, because that movie may have been for a certain audience, or budgeting was restricted or the location manager just wasn't well enough informed. There can be other reasons.

The mountains of Alaska, British Columbia, Alberta, Montana, Utah, northern Wyoming and California, due to altitude, climate and fault lines may all manifest different physical characteristics. Obviously, the Alps would differ from the Himalayas, you see where I'm going with this.

Though, for the record, there are parts of Montana where the mountains look similar to Alaska. And others have some distinct features.

You could consider these concepts in terms of second unit for locations.

In *The Bourne Legacy*, there was a scene that takes place in an old home in the northeast, in the fall, no less. Something about this location really bothered me. The story, stunts, editing, pacing were all terrific, but there was something I couldn't put my finger on.

It was the foliage, fall, the location…it was all wrong. There's nothing sexy about fall and colorful leaves. When you think about *Bourne* or the *Bond* movies you think sex appeal, exotic locations… not your grandmother's house! Robert Ludlum was the writer of the successful *Bourne* series, but I believe it was another writer who finished *Legacy*. It's in the details…

In the next chapter you'll find that I do integrate the location in the Action Design. Except this isn't necessarily for mood or feel, but for speed…

Action Design

Action design is a new term for something that has been around for some time, unwittingly. Not sure about the etymology of the words, but for as long as there have been stunts, there has been a form of action design.

As I mentioned in another chapter, in Hong Kong cinema, they may spend two months on one action scene. Wire work, fight choreography, camera placement can all be encompassed by action design. Also, I might add, in Asia, an action director or fight director may get equal billing to the director. Some go to see a movie just for the fight director, not the director or even the story or actors!

This has really evolved over the last few years. Different stunt coordinators or action directors may bring in different forms of what we call action design. Each of these people may have different strengths or even weaknesses. I've seen a "fight guy" do a car chase and a "car guy" do a fight sequence. You can see the differences. Their familiarity with the various disciplines will manifest based on the complexity of a particular scene.

There is a big-time stunt coordinator who does a lot of high-end action sequences, but when I see his work, I can tell he's a natural motorcycle guy. It's all beautiful, but the car work is a little forced. Mind you, a lot of this is in the writing for the stunt coordinators and generally it's their job to execute.

I mean, look at *Fast and Furious 8*. Vin Diesel went from a street thug to being a super-agent who drives his car in Siberia over a submarine with explosions and "stuff." Of course that's a world-class stunt team, but the weak link in this case is the writing.

The car chase has changed the last couple of years. It's now using movements that are generally not car movements but movements using "rigging," essentially wires. As a result, the cars themselves are manipulated, creating a bit of spinning effect. In other words, the motion mimics a kick or a punch.

When I saw *Baby Driver*, the tempo, rhythm and editing led me to believe that this was a music video with car stuff *in* it. Because of the song, insert shots had to be put in to give more punch to the chase. In my opinion, this isn't a car chase, but a car sequence.

What I will call the golden age of car chases ended with *Ronin*.

For *Ronin*, Frankenheimer employed 200 rally drivers – rally drivers are amazing drivers, but they may not even be stunt drivers – they have different skill sets, and essentially this element can be used in action design.

The car chase has been evolving ever since: *Bourne Supremacy*, *Quantum of Solace*, *Safe House*, *Mad Max: Fury Road* were all great examples of that, and are also some of my own favorites for various reasons.

If you were to ask stunt coordinators, second-unit directors and action directors what action design is, I believe you'd get different responses depending on their backgrounds (fighting, car, motorcycle, fire, wirework/rigging, etc.).

This is from Jeff Habberstad, 2nd unit director of *Ironman 3, Dr. Strange* and the *Antman* series, his take on action design:

What have I learned about action design over the years? I would say number one is to surround yourself with a great team. If your ego tells you that you are good enough to cover for an "ok" team, you will lose. No one is great at everything. The action world has evolved, where the Stunt Coordinator does not just "put together" a fight any more. Hire a great fight choreographer. Hire a great Stunt Rigger. Hire the most talented performers. Equally important is collaboration. Many coordinators will not involve their top crew members in aspects of developing the action. They will go alone to meetings, they will be the only one on distribution lists for script, schedules, previz, etc. Take your crew with you, get them first hand information that you can take back and discuss. The final product will only get better. Unless you are the one I have never met, who is perfect.

All these are worth the battle you may incur with production. I have never been not hired back for spending too much on a great result, but the opposite has happened to me and many others.

We may not be working on a $100 million movie but the essence here is have a great team and communication is key!

I also spoke with fighter extraordinaire, 2nd unit director, and stunt coordinator J.J. Perry. J.J. is a combat veteran with a 138 amateur fights under his belt. He's seen some real action and that ALWAYS helps in this process.

If you have seen, *X-Men* (Origins), *Old Boy* (remake), or the John Wick series...you've seen his work. I can recall the first time watching his work. There's something very punishing about his sequences. As time went on I was able to notice JJ's work or style. First thing, in his process...every move has to matter. No telegraphing it. The audience doesn't know it's coming...

Efficient fighting or ass-kicking is more like it! There's no staging. It just goes down! Let me explain... if there is a table, he will use it. If there is a bottle...he will use it. Guerilla with his artistry. But this is where it gets interesting. He will use the edge of the table...hitting his "bullet points" as he said. Maybe the hero is down and out and all you have is that bottle. Maybe he sticks it in his ear...then stomps on it! It's lights out. He doesn't deny it's violent, but it does give more impact to the sequence. That's his job to keep the audience interested. It's a bit of shock factor. Producers pay him a lot of money to get people in the seats...

The second thing he talks about is the venue. Sort of the environment, if you will.
For *John Wick* there's hallways, or the catacombs in *John Wick 2*. So he'll design the sequences in that proximity of space...or lack of. That will encompass what weapons or fight aspects of it.
Remember...efficiency. John Wick, the character, is a one man shop of badassery!

What I wasn't aware of is that J.J. and some mutual friends all started around the same time - David Leitch, Garrett Warren, and Chad Stahwelski. They were all ex-fighters in different weight classes. You look at their IMDB's and these are the current top hombres. They have been in the business for a long time. These skills and such didn't come overnight.

A couple of things I might add is that before he gets into his process for an upcoming film, JJ watches John Woo's "hallway sequence" in *Hard Boiled*. If you haven't seen it...that sequence is a masterclass in filmmaking.

There's a lot of similarities in his process as mine. What's key here is his point of view as a man and as an artist.

Lastly, one thing that you may come to a surprise is that all of us edit, either on set or after filming. Garrett does his own edits, I do, Spiro Razatos has his guys. It's a key component in action, as sound design is. If the edit is not "on," the action design and the artistry can go awry.

I have been very fortunate to have been able to work with masters and ask stupid questions. So, when I see something being done... I may do it differently and not necessarily the "right" way. My own background might compensate for it – my experience in shooting, editing, production design, location, for example. You can do the same.

Where I trained, top stunt coordinators and second unit directors would come out and give us workshops, and there was a lot of fighting stuff. They might not have had the most amazing resumes or IMDB listing, but they had been doing the job for over twenty years, and some may even have been ex-fighters. They each had their own team and approach. I cannot begin to tell you how blessed I have been to be in that position to be able to see and experience these phenomenal performers. It has been key. There were many different ways or styles that gave me a lot of ideas as to how I would approach a fight sequence.

There's a fellow who came out the last few years, an ex-previs (pre-visualization) guy like me. He got his shot and has done memorable work by creating some amazing fight teams with various styles and backgrounds, but what I want to stress here is one of his latest fight sequences. He shot it himself. Why do you think that is?

His action design was based partly on shooting it himself. He may have had some else shoot it, and as a result the final product would not have been the same. Maybe the producers were breathing down his neck demanding this or that... or it could have been he designed it exactly with his camera moves in mind. It's integrated.

Sometimes you have to work on your strengths based on *your* background. Not all action guys have action backgrounds. The second unit director in *Gone in 60 Seconds* is a camera guy; Alexander Witt, who has done a lot of the *Bond* films is also a camera guy. These guys are going to do it how they know or want to do it...

Editing may shape the movie or sequence, but it's the camera that is the bottleneck. If you don't get it into the camera, you're dead, it doesn't matter how amazing the stunt is!

If you look at the difference between a Stephen Spielberg movie and a Clint Eastwood flick it's generally the size of the canvas, so to speak. Both are captured on camera. Spielberg's *Saving Private Ryan* for example, or Christopher Nolan's *Dunkirk* have huge canvasses with a lot of details. Eastwood's work uses a much smaller canvas, but essentially gets the same story in the camera. Eastwood is one of the only directors in Hollywood who comes out under time and under budget – he is a very efficient filmmaker. He's a no-frills guy who always uses the same people. Spielberg can include every detail because he has the money and the time. I'm not taking anything from Mr. Spielberg, I'm just illustrating a point: if you don't have the money, you have to be creative about how you get it *in* the camera.

Now, a stunt sometimes lasts only a second or two, maybe three seconds, but the amount of planning and costs could be through the roof! You want to be smart about how you budget, plan or structure that into the sequence.

For me, having collaborators or guidance from some of the best action people who are not "action guys" per se, but have worked at the highest level in action has been just as valuable in the learning process. Editing (thank you Rick Pearson), sound design (thank you Chris Smith & Paula Fairfield) and sound mixing (thank you Bob Beemer), in my opinion, are essential in bringing life to action or stunts. Watch a fight sequence or car chase without sound and see how much less value it brings to the table. CGI will enhance the stunt or fix its weakness, but I see CGI like taking a pill, whereas the basics are the basics. The physics are getting pretty close with new technologies in CGI, but generally audiences know. That may change in the next few years, but I will stand by that for now. Funny thing though, *Bullitt* is still considered to have one of the best car chases of all time, and it's fifty years old!

Coming to Europe opened my eyes to a whole new world. Some of the villages, roads, etc. are hundreds if not thousands of years old. Not to mention all the texture they have. Cars have only been around for 100 years or so.

The way I scout in Europe is very different from what I do in North America, Asia or Africa. The "design" is different. Because of the design of European towns, backgrounds and roads are different, so I can manipulate the environment for more speed. Not to mention Europe has that exotic "feel." Look at the *Bourne, Bond* and *Mission Impossible* series. These aren't done in Kansas for a reason. Of course, tax credits and incentives are a factor, but the audience has certain expectations of these brands, they want to be taken to far-away places. We give them X number of dollars, euros, yuan, and they take us to a foreign land… and hopefully we see some cool shit along the way!

I've been traveling abroad the last few years, and I have seen a *lot* of things. For the first year or so, my mind was constantly on action design, as there are so many things to work off of. Because I am aware of the various tools of the trade, so to speak, understanding stunts or the physics of such can make for a wonderland of creation and exploration.

Some countries in the EU have real advantages and loopholes for doing some amazing things. Some don't even know about their own loopholes. That's your advantage!

It was interesting, maybe even a boyhood dream, to visit the locales of all my favorite action sequences: the opening sequence from *Quantum of Solace* (Lake Garda area) and its fight sequence (Siena), the opening of *Bourne Ultimatum* (Waterloo station, London), the running/fight sequence of *Bourne Supremacy* (Tangiers) and the Mini sequence in *Bourne Identity* (Paris), the car chases in *Ronin* (Paris and Nice), the motorbike sequence in *Skyfall* (Istanbul), the fight sequence at the end of *Casino Royal* (Venice)… I could go on. It was all friggin' AWESOME!

I've seen hundreds of churches, cathedrals, museums, art pieces, etc. But there is something that you have in the movies that can't be found anywhere else. It's the dream itself...

When I started out in stunts I wasn't sure about the sequence, so I'd reach out to the stunt coordinator, DP, editor or location manager, whatever relationship I had available to me. As time went on, my own skills developed, and this is a vital point I'm making here: if you don't know how, figure out another way or use something else to fix it! Once you have an idea of the various departments, you'll have the ability to figure it out. Sometimes you need to have an actual stunt team, preferably a group who have worked with each other and really know each other's skills. Another important resource can be just knowing the mechanics of filmmaking so that you can create the illusion. Of course knowing or having both is ideal, but not always possible. Throwing money at it is not always the solution.

These are literally the differences between independent film and advertising or branded content. Independent films do not explore how to do stunts or action because they don't have the budget. For example, doing a car crash off-screen is not necessarily cheaper than a simple fight sequence. Advertising people rely on the creative director for the brief, and the client doesn't have the evaluation skills to know different. Neither is experienced in filmmaking or even speed for that matter. Of course, not every commercial or branded content spot has to look like it's from an action film, but these concepts are not integrated in the sense of how it is constructed, so essentially it makes something that is not only forgettable but ends up being costly too! Then they hire a regular production company to do the action. That's like bringing parking enforcement to fight terrorists! You need special forces commandos. They have the skills to get the job done. Get the idea?

Maybe four or five years ago, I approached a premium British car company, and frankly I was getting sick of sand being kicked in my face by marketing. So, I asked these gentlemen to name for me five memorable car commercials. Blank stares. I said, ok then, three memorable spots. Blink blink. One?! Nothing. Then I said, name five favorite car chases. They couldn't get it out fast enough! Why is that?

"Screw the dialogue... lets wreck some cars." - Hal Needham

Story schmory...

Do your homework!

Frame Rates

There has been a lot of talk about frame rates by James Cameron, Peter Jackson and others, but the biggest proponent has been Hollywood VFX legend and pioneer Douglas Trumbull.

These master filmmakers have used their insights with the intention of creating a better experience for the viewer. Mr. Trumbull developed Showscan, which shoots at 60 frames per second (fps). He claimed that biometric testing of audiences showed a more emotional response. Jackson and Cameron wanted to use 48 fps. Jackson used that in *The Hobbit*. Trumbull created another visual technology that is 3D – 4K at 120 fps, which also is projected at 120 fps – and called it Magi.

We're talking about action or second unit though, and there should be a purpose for shooting at higher than 24 fps.

I see a lot of music videos now where they shoot a large portion of them at high frame rates. Just like in the *Bourne* action sequences, this is something that can be used to create an effect for a scene, not the entire movie or video.

I am a little disappointed that the manufacturers are dictating the aesthetics of frame rates. Even when I asked veterans why they used a particular frame rate, more often than not it was because that's the max they could do on their cameras. The Phantom, RED, Arri and Sony are leading the way in that department, whereas Twixtor and other programs are done in post, but there is give-and-take when doing something in post, namely, interpolation.* Note: this may be dated by publication, there are plenty of other programs out there.

There have been other filmmakers who used these creative opportunities, but they did it for impact and thought it out first. Examples are Dziga Vertov's *Man with the Movie Camera* and Akira Kurosawa's *Seven Samurai*.

Sam Peckinpah was so famous for shooting the action sequences in *The Getaway* and *Cross of Iron* at 66 fps that some Hollywood vets will say to "Peckinpah that shot." John Woo has picked up where Peckinpah left off with *Hardboiled*, *Faceoff*, etc. They have been creating a style in the director's vision.

Then there is Kubrick with *The Shining*. There's a particular scene where the blood comes out of the elevator that is shot at 144 fps. That was researched, discussed, it was well thought out. You see, this wasn't about turning on the button and now it looks cool because it's slow-mo!

The sequence in the *Matrix* called "bullet time" (it's the first slow-mo sequence, when the cameras go around Carrie-Anne Moss) is shot at 150 fps. Again, it was discussed at length.

Just like you need to know *where* and *why* you position the camera, you also need to know *why* you chose *that*

---

* Mathematical calculations used to determine what values a given pixel should have based on the values of its neighbors. For example, let's say an image is scaled up in size. There aren't enough pixels of data to fill in the new image size, so the computer is often instructed to try and figure out what pixel values would seem reasonable to fill in the gaps. It does this through a process of interpolation or resampling. There are different algorithms used to perform such interpolation.

frame rate. Obviously, with film it was easier, but we are almost there with digital cameras.

Suppose you see a shot of three sexy women on the dance floor with short tight dresses getting their groove on, as one example, and another shot of a woman putting on stockings slowwwwwly. There's a good chance that the three dancing women I speak of are beautiful, and the one stocking shot emphasizes only the leg. The women dancing have a harmonized sexiness and the woman putting on a stocking is a little sultry. Both scenes are meant to have sex appeal, but the frame rate could forward the story as well as create more impact to the shot. And it could be the frame rate is changed just on a shot, as an insert into the sequence.

In the original *The Getaway* action sequences, the tight editing also created exciting memorable sequences. This was Peckinpah's trademark. You can create a style, but it's nice to have the freedom to create something new each time.

In John Frankenheimer's *Grand Prix*, there are three race sequences throughout the movie, and each one had a completely different style. *This* is filmmaking. Nowadays theme and style can be used throughout, and in some cases this is extremely effective depending on the genre and story.

Editing

Editing is such a big deal that it can make or break a movie.

Spiro Razatos's work on *Fast and Furious* are generally his second unit edits. He was not the primary editor for the movie. He directed and had on-site edits to see how the shots worked. He had to do this for previs as well, so as to get "approval" for the sequence.

You can't talk action without talking about the *Bourne* movies. This style of movie making or editing changed the way we make movies. I believe the first time I saw the shaky cam look was in the movie *The Rock* with Sean Connery and Nicolas Cage, and the first time I saw quick edits was in Sam Peckinpah's *Wild Bunch*. It was quite jarring to my senses at the time and took some time to adjust to. The editing with the *Bourne* series and the shaky cam created new sensibilities. Now, when the young guys ask me to "shoot it like *Bourne*," I know what they mean.

In the past, that style of shooting had a purpose: it would be used in a scene to create confusion. It would never to be used for entire action sequences.

The jury is still out on some of these movies, especially if I listen to my editor, DP, stunt friends, but personally, I loved the action sequences for this reason alone. What I feel was done here was these scenes were wrung out in their entirety in terms of the action and sensations.

I had the chance to speak with editor extraordinaire Rick Pearson specifically about the car sequence at the end of *The Bourne Supremacy*. Rick felt the collaboration was so seamless that when he presented it to 2nd unit/ action director Dan Bradley, Dan said, "It was like you were in my head." That's a huge honor, and I would safely assume that this is the reason they've continued their relationship ever since. They are currently working together on *Wonder Woman 2*.

If you have ever been involved in any dangerous activity, you know that things are not black and white. You are going for it, and there really aren't any rules other than survival.

The characters in the *Bourne* movies are elite assassins, not run-of-the-mill special forces types. They don't need to flex their muscles, they just have an objective: to finish their mission. Jason Bourne lost his memory, and as a creative choice, this required dynamic filmmaking.

What the *Bourne* movies never really got credit for was the ebb and flow of the action. The drama was a little tense, since he didn't know what was going on, and when all hell broke loose, it turned into some of the best action sequences of all time.

Bradley's best work, in my opinion, was in *Quantum of Solace*. The opening sequence is sheer brilliance, and the following fight/chase sequence in the church was just as clever. However, it's the editing, sound design and stunt directing/coordinating that set those scenes apart. I will talk further about the opening sequence from *Quantum* in the chapter titled "Cars."

Juxtaposition was key between the slower-paced scenes and the faster-paced ones. What hadn't been done before was to have *really* short edits, like 8-15 frames per cut. Considering 24 fps (as discussed in the previous chapter), that's a third or half a second for each cut! My hunch is that what people may complain about is that they essentially can't process visual information that fast. Times have changed, and sensibilities have followed.

I've seen *The Bourne Ultimatum* multiple times, but a recent viewing of it actually bothered my eyes, which isn't something that had occurred before. It could be for a variety of reasons, perhaps being tired, my eyes being sore from looking at something close up or the distance between screen and myself. Filmmakers actually consider this beforehand, and the trick is to cater to the audience. I believe James Cameron has even developed formulas for this.

For *The Bourne Legacy* with Jeremy Renner, I could spot the insert shots clear as a day, and I made note of this. The inserts shots were so pale in comparison to the first-unit shots that I thought they were actually using GoPros. In actual fact, they had used Canon 5D Mark II. The difference between the Arri Alexa and the Canon 5D was so dramatic in terms of quality that it was actually jarring to me.

However most people don't really notice these things (insert shots) because the pacing/action is so dominant that they just get caught up in the scene. Even in the last couple of years, we have now more options in terms of cameras.

Skyfall, which was beautifully shot, was slower-paced than the previous *Bond* film *Quantum of Solace*. I could literally see where the camera was placed as I was watching the movie. Granted, my eyes are trained to see such, as I have developed this skill being right in the heart of the action.

That's the difference between someone who is concerned with craft services being moved an extra 100 feet and what they call a "camera man who doesn't mind getting dirty." If you are willing to get your hands "dirty" or stick your neck out, so to speak, you'll have a greater understanding of shooting action, and you'll be more able to perceive what is really going on. Your eyes can be further developed by working with other trained professionals. As a result, if editing is done right, you can create something very raw and visceral.

A scene can move fast in several ways, including without rapid cutting to create tension. *Drive* was a great example of this. The opening sequence has nothing but tension, and you are literally on the edge of your seat, because you don't know what's going to happen. It's just a short burst, but the crescendo that was built up to that point was a testament to creative, beautiful filmmaking.

What's the difference between a *Bourne* movie and *Drive*? Well, the average length of the shot of the dramatic movie is three seconds or more, and I'm willing to bet that second-unit shots are less, and in *Bourne*'s case, even more so. Did both movies have tension when things were about to go down? Absolutely.

Sound design is a big part of this, and it will have its own chapter.

I had a great conversation about action with the editor of *Die Hard*, Frank Urioste. A good friend shared with me that Frank's background was in music. Frank trained as a sound engineer, but there were no jobs at the time, and he had some other options in terms of career paths. Obviously, he made the right choice when he became an editor. It was his background of music, understanding beats, etc. that helped him. He was able to influence the editing to create probably one of the most successful action movies of the time, also catapulting Bruce Willis's career. There's a definite tempo to *Die Hard* that you can feel.

Rick Pearson (*Bourne, Bond, Kong: Skull Island, Wonder Woman 2*) enlightened me to the fact that a lot of editors have music backgrounds. As the drummer is the musician who drives the beat, it would be a good parallel to think of the editor as driving the beat and rhythm for the sequence.

Watching the chase sequence in *Safe House* with Denzel Washington and Ryan Reynolds was the first time that I couldn't predict what was going to happen in a car chase. That scene defied my expectations, because often I can figure things out beforehand, based on various clues and tempo, from my understanding of filmmaking, stunts and physics.

What Rick pointed out to me was, in the filmmaking, they intentionally established a specific point of view. The car chase takes place from Ryan Reynold's P.O.V., as he plays the newbie in the field, whereas Denzel's character was a crafty veteran. As a result, all Ryan's character could do was react. That's exactly how the car chase was edited to feel to the viewer.

Matt Damon's character in the *Bourne* series, in contrast, is a highly proficient assassin who would always have plenty of options, and who wouldn't do something based on emotion, due to being trained for any kind of scenario. So you can see how in these two films, the car chase editing would work on a different logic.

So, when shooting an action sequence, it will save you a lot of time to know in terms of what shots you need and *why*.

With *Quantum of Solace*, Mr. Pearson was influenced by director Marc Forster, who wanted something "fractured and impressionistic." I would say they attained that. If you weren't on the edge of your seat after the first two action sequences, I would suggest you check for a pulse!

Some of these projects were so big that Rick would want the dailies (footage) from second unit everyday, if possible, so as to stay abreast of what's happening. For this reason alone, he was always aware of the second unit's vision.

Mr. Pearson mentioned this word before: intention. If he's staying current with what's going on when he edits the sequence, and works it into the main body, he'll have the *intention* of the character dialed in. Key.

Rick is also aware of the franchise style/theme, if you will. He won't parrot it, but he'll certainly factor in past elements. This is also key. Rick is comfortable with what he's doing based on his understanding of the story and process. His point of view on the artistry is very sound.

But Hollywood sometimes will try to take these elements away from you...

If we copied everything, nothing would ever change. There is no such thing as the right way, only *your* way.

We can't consider editing without mentioning Walter Murch (*Apocalypse Now*). One of Walter's trademarks is that matched action isn't as important (matched action means that if an arm is in the air for a single shot, the next shot cannot show the arm down). The emotion of the scene is senior. Again, for Murch, the better shot would be the one that was stronger emotionally.

Another iconic movie is *High Noon*. It was shot as a love story and re-edited; and considered to be one of the best westerns of all time. Everything came down to the last few minutes, and Elmo Williams edited it to the music so as to build tension. They gave him the Oscar for that.

I was discussing some shots and edits from the movie *Bird* with a friend of mine who used to write and edit for Clint Eastwood. They were going over some shots, and Clint asked my friend what the best shot was. Clint says the actors *always* pick certain shots and claimed that Forrest Whittaker had picked the same one. The point I'm making with this anecdote is you have to know why you pick a certain shot: does it fit the story, does it add to the culture of it, etc.

I've read quite a few biographies of Clint and I know people who work with him. He's a no-nonsense kind of guy. No frills. Even when shooting, he's not overly concerned with the placement of practicals (a practical could be a lamp in a scene). It's redundant. I can recall from one of his interviews that in *Pale Rider*, the lighting was poor, but he wanted it that way because the character's face had already been seen, and he felt it wasn't necessary to reveal the face *all* the time. He has some shooting techniques that are very simple too. He's a very efficient filmmaker.

What I'm saying here is sometimes you don't have to get too fancy.

Personally, I feel Rick Pearson was instrumental in the way we edit/make movies. I would also add that Rick, in a quick but classy fashion, would pass the credit to his colleagues, as he did with Christopher Rouse, Dan Bradley and Paul Greengrass.

When I asked Rick who his favorite directors were, he mentioned "Danny Boyle." He stressed that it didn't matter who was editing, that his work is not overworked and feels appropriate. We spoke about David Fincher's work, that Fincher is extremely talented and that his work is very clear. One of the things I got from Rick was that if the collaboration between editor and director is clear, it'll manifest in the final product.

Another factor in editing, especially when the footage or talent isn't that good, is the editor can be your friend.

When I saw the opening sequence of *The Grandmaster* (based on the life of Ip man), it was nothing short of spectacular... but there was something I felt was still missing. Here we are, talking about one of the best fight coordinators of all time, the legendary Woo Ping, and a brilliant filmmaker, Wong Kar Wai, and one of the biggest stars out of Hong Kong, Tony Leung. What I saw, I believe, was that the rain, being darkly lit, combined with the editing, obscured the footage and was used as subterfuge. In other words, Tony Leung can't fight.

Somebody else may not see that, but soon after, I spoke to a friend of mine who claimed Tony couldn't fight, and that explained the other factors. Yup, a good editor can do wonders... in both realms.

Conversely, it was still done well because of all the competent department heads. Can you imagine if the guy could fight?

Another factor in editing, in terms of responsibility, is the quick edis, *especially* using light. Yes, I did say responsibility. Let me explain.

There's a great song from the late 1980s from N.I.N. (Nine Inch Nails). A young brilliant filmmaker by the name of Harris Savides shot the video for it, "Head

Like a Hole." Let me state for the record, this is an amazing song, but no one can get through the video without their head hurting! It's more like an MKUltra experiment.[*] This was at the pinnacle of music videos.

Lastly, for action or second unit…the editing can be specialized, and as a result, key.

If you were in need of something with some punch, I would lean in the direction of a trailer editor. The trailer is what gets people into the seats in the theatre! You have two or so minutes to get their attention and get them to *show up*.

If not, it wouldn't be a bad idea to bring in the stunt coordinator for a few hours, as they were instrumental in designing the sequence. What they envisioned doesn't always translate into a good final product. In fact, you'll find that they are rarely happy with their creations. Somehow, the cuts are never what they had in mind. Further, just between you and me… if you bring in the stunt coordinator to the edit, and I assure you, you've made a friend for life. Plus, their trained eyes will make the most out of the scene. This is a win-win situation.

Studios spend an exorbitant amount of money to create trailers. They may hire half a dozen companies to come up with something and in the end hybrid them together. These shots are quite short, so it takes some skill to put that all together in such a way that evokes the emotion that you are trying to achieve.

What's the most memorable trailer that got you to go to the theatre to watch a movie?

---

[*] http://en.wikipedia.org/wiki/Project_MKUltra

Sound Design

I can't stress enough the importance of sound design, especially with action. Truthfully, sound design is just as important in other genres, but the difference between action and other genres is the length of the shot: action shots are short. Sound designers are making the imagery more memorable and evoking a response. Sound design, in my opinion, is what gives action visceral impact.

Think about these memorable movie sounds: a punch in the face or body, tires skidding, a gunshot a la spaghetti western. Ennio Morricone almost single-handedly changed sound design. And with Sergio Leone's gun fighting stance, it made for interesting viewing. The combination made an impression on my mind many years ago.

Sometimes the sound design was cheesy in the past, like the 1970s kung fu movies using automated dialogue replacement (ADR), which means recording audio after the visuals were shot so they were generally out of sync.

Meanwhile, in the TV show *Dukes of Hazzard,* you hear the sound of tires screeching on dirt. This is not possible folks, but since the show lacked depth, this gave it more punch, so to speak.

A couple of years back, I was watching some fireworks. It was the hundredth anniversary of the town, and so the display was a little more special than the typical fireworks display. What I noticed, like clockwork, was that when the fireworks went off, the audience always responded with an "ewww." When the sound went off, the response was always "awww." The funny thing was that the response was universal.

For the very young kids it was a little more upbeat for the fact that it may have been the first time they were seeing fireworks. Whereas somebody older may have seen fireworks countless times, so it really didn't have the same impact.

In the late 90s, when I was living in Vancouver, B.C. the city had fireworks displays that were competitions between three countries, capping the event with a grand finale that combined the efforts of all three countries. This was really amazing, as they synchronized the fireworks with music, and pacing/tempo was also considered in the competition. Moreover, the fireworks were, sometimes, shaped. The fact that 500,000 people would show up was a testament to what aesthetics can do for the psyche or soul.

Well, this is no different to action and sound design. The image comes up, but it's just the image, and it can only be experienced visually, but it takes the sound to receive it sonically, and to some degree tactically, due to receiving the aural punch from it.

Move forward to a movie theatre. The projector, screen and speakers are continually calibrated to maximize the experience. Some theatres have even been redesigned to make the entire theatre resonate on the effect.

Cinerama was popular in the 1950s to early 1970s, but the cost of shooting it was off the charts. Here the effect was visual stimulation that was, frankly, epic. The audience was immersed in the grand landscape.

Sound design triggers the mind in such a way as to evoke a response.

If you were to look at a wavelength with a centerline going through it, there would be two parts. Half of the wave is on each side of the centerline. Now imagine that closer to the centerline would be dialogue and working towards the outer areas you are getting into sound design.

Within that range, after dialogue, there is room for layering with Foley work. Foley is the reproduction of everyday sound effects. The Foley artist will create the ambience of the mood or sequence. For example, a Foley trick would be putting cornstarch in a leather pouch to recreate the sound of snow crunching. Another is a shaking pair of gloves to sound like bird wings flapping.

Then would come sound design.

So, it would be like this, roughly: audio from the actors, Foley work and then sound design. There may be slight nuances, and someone working in this field would probably write a lecture on the differences, but for argument's sake, these actions give life to the visuals.

Someone has said that sound design is the creation of sounds from scratch, whereas Foley are sounds that are recorded from the environment, such as footsteps, doors closing, etc.

In *Quantum of Solace*, in the opening sequence and the introduction of the new Aston Martin, every time 007 shifts, you hear *ching-ching* or *clunk-clunk*. There is *no* Aston Martin on the planet that sounds like that, but the movement needed emphasis because of all the action that was going on around it. It's a tribute to Jean-Pierre Melville, in my opinion.

As I mentioned in "Editing," this opening sequence is a masterpiece, and one of the reasons is that it starts at the very beginning. Something that is not too common, the sound starts with the MGM lion growling, then continues with the Columbia statue, all the while this ominous sound leads to a visual: a helicopter shot, in which the music becomes dramatic and is interlaced with inserts of what is to come. As the helicopter gets closer to the event, the music builds up to a crescendo and all hell breaks loose, then Bond does his thing. Just describing it makes me feel all warm and fuzzy.

It's brilliant, as your imagination of what is to come is being exercised vividly. I have probably watched the opening sequence a few hundred times. It's like a drug…and the hair is still standing up on my arms.

That's pure film-making, or should I say sound-making!

Editing and sound design go hand-and-hand. You may have the ultimate stunt/sequence but without the sound, you are lacking half of the experience. It's *that* experience that starts resonating within your mind and what those sounds mean to you.

Another great example of this is the helicopter scene in *Goodfellas* with the different songs being intercut within the main song. Sound design, in combination with editing and pacing, uses this to evoke different subplots within the story. Masterfully done.

If there were one thing to continue researching, it would be sound design. Just like the camera is the bottleneck to the stunt, sound design is the bottleneck to your senses or perceptions. A trailer editor can make the most of that. If you have sound designers who do it every day, I'm sure, they'd make the experience as different as night and day.

A good friend of mine, D. Chris Smith, is one of the top sound designers in business (*Revenant, John Wick 2,* etc.). This is what he said regarding sound design for action:

"Sound design, or specifically sound effects, editing, recording, and mixing, is the art of telling the story through sound.

A C4 explosion, a Glock 17 gunshot, a big face punch, a sword whoosh, or a 2018 Bugatti Chiron engine rev could all be sounds the designer uses to paint the world our ears hear... transporting the viewer to a different world and supporting the onscreen events.

In case of most action-based projects, little to none of the actual onset production sound can be used (due to excessive noise, coverage, or even to just stay off camera). Therefore, everything must be recreated in post-production. In the case of vehicles, for instance, the actual car might be provided with a stunt driver, trailered to the desert, staged with special microphones in the engine compartment and on the tail pipe... and all the movements of the vehicle would be meticulously recorded for placement to picture by the sound designer later in post. This process would apply to most real world events, anything from ambiences, guns, people, vehicles to animals.

The sound designer would utilize these new sounds recorded in the 'field', to sculpt, weave and craft the aural experience so the viewer is practically put into the scene... Evoking tension, emotions and ultimately believing what they're watching.

Sound, in the simplest terms, is half of the viewing experience. Visuals being the other half. The two work in tandem, and have to work harmoniously making the performance, truly unforgettable."

Solid! Take note…

Music

"A film is – or should be – more like music than like fiction. It should be a progression of moods and feelings. The theme, what's behind the emotion, the meaning, all that comes later." - Stanley Kubrick

This is one of the chapters I've most anticipated and most wanted to talk about. I have always been passionate about music and probably would have taken a different path if not for my background and inclination toward other interests. Before I got into the film industry, as a moviegoer, it was the music that always hit home with me. "Sunshine of Your Love" in *Goodfellas*, "The End" in *Apocalypse Now*, Al Green in *Dead Presidents*, Eric Clapton at the end of *Phenomenon*. How about that song in *Ferris Bueller's Day Off*… "Oh Yeah!" These songs, at those given moments, just hit a nerve, and the timing up to that point was of critical essence. Obviously there has been other music that is memorable. Can you remember the themes for *Star Wars* or *2001: A Space Odyssey*?

As mentioned earlier, I recently asked some folks to name their favorite car commercial. Everyone, and I mean everyone, could not recall even one. However, when I mentioned the Cadillac commercial that used the Led Zeppelin song "Rock and Roll," their body/tone transformed right before my eyes. That commercial aired in 2002! How could somebody remember that commercial, clear as day, and yet couldn't remember a commercial from the past weekend, or even a Super Bowl commercial, for that matter? It was the music in this case. It was sheer brilliance. Cadillac was looking for a new image and wanted to get rid of their "older man" association. If you were a teenager in the late '70s, when Zeppelin were considered gods in the music world, that would put you in the late 30s to early 40s category in the early 2000s, which was the target audience of that ad. Moreover, at that age, you generally had a bit of money saved up, something in a 401k (retirement fund), possibly a family, yet still have some oomph left, as well as remembering the prestige that Cadillac carried. It was exactly the right song for the target demographic.

A song or bit of music can add so much more to the visual experience. I mentioned the helicopter sequence from *Goodfellas* for this reason, and there is not a man I know who doesn't recall that scene. I could even say it is something of a legend. Yes, I am saying it! Can you recall some songs that hit home for you? I recall listening to the AC/DC album *If You Want Blood You've Got It.* What I realized, which is worth noting, is that I had heard the album a few hundred times by that point, but the word "unleashed," and later on, the word "RAW" came to mind. I have great admiration for musicians because they have to practice... a lot. If they don't practice, they go out of sync and sound sloppy. Moreover, when playing live, the stakes are higher, and in this particular album, each musician was *just going for it*! The thing about this versus filmmaking is that in filmmaking, you can always get another take.

Music, it's not so easy when live. Music can capture the mood that something visual may not be able to. If you were to listen to the Sex Pistols, Edith Piaf, Black Sabbath, N.W.A., Sly and the Family Stone, Nirvana or Mozart, there would be something resonating with you that can't be gotten with the medium we refer to as film. For this reason, music can definitely complement what you are trying to convey to the audience.

One such sequence that caught my attention in terms of filmmaking was the opening dance in *Blade*. What I would like to stress here is the matching of "harmonics." What is the definition? What's interesting is the closest thing I could find was from something from 1828! To me, this is a confirmation of how we have lost our way with technology. To simplify, it's the harmony of sounds *and* vibrations, but for mixing or for music to cohere[*] with a visual medium, they need total agreement with each other.

In the opening sequence of *Blade*, the editing, lighting, strobing, interspersed with higher frame rates, complemented the music well and essentially matched the harmonics of the visual aspects. The effect was compounded, because it was the opening scene where the tone and story were revealed. If any of those aspects were a little off, in terms of frequencies or wavelengths, it just wouldn't have the same impact. You may not see it, but you will feel or perceive it.

Can you recall a time when you were young where you heard a song in a movie, and it just hit a nerve? The very first time I heard "Stranglehold" by Ted Nugent, I was sitting in a little fishing boat in Northern Ontario. We were fishing for pickerel – the best-tasting freshwater fish, for the record. It was twilight, and bats were swooping by, trying to get at our bait. And in the distance, it must have been almost a mile away, was this massive house with music blaring – "Stranglehold." It was a little surreal, and almost an unbelievable set of circumstances. It created a great and everlasting memory...

---

[*] Have internal elements or parts logically connected so that aesthetic consistency results (Courtesy of MacMillan dictionary).

Invincible is a 2006 movie with Mark Wahlberg as a bartender turned football pro. He had struggled through training camp and looked like he was a flop. The filmmakers decided at a certain moment that the character overcame his struggles and *right* at that moment they used the song "Stranglehold." The timing was so perfect that the hair on the back of my neck stood up! As a directorial decision, a crane shot could have been used, as it was a turning point, but the music had far more impact.

Back in 2011, en route to a shoot in Colorado, I was coming upon Monument Valley. There was a lightning storm and it was truly amazing! There, "Stranglehold" came on the airwaves, and instead of pulling over to take some shots, I got caught up in the moment, as the overall harmonic and visual experience evoked a certain feeling. Another time I was cave hunting in Texas… again, the song came on. These were memorable times for me. Not just listening to the radio, sitting in a metal coffin on the I-405 in rush hour.

It could be the day your kid was born, when your favorite sports team won the championship, when you lost your virginity, when you were out drinking with your buddies, or in my case fishing on a little boat in the middle of nowhere. Hell, I don't even like fishing, but the memory is everlasting. Ultimately you are trying to create an experience for the viewer. For me, this is one of my favorite parts… Hopefully you can appreciate this as much as I do.

On a side note, to broaden your scope of music, here's an anecdote to consider: a friend of mine, an accomplished award-winning musician, was travelling around Turkey learning about music, and she was having a rough time, as they construct music in different systems than we do in the west. As a result, she has had to *relearn* how to make music or, even more fundamentally, relearn how to learn. I feel that music in some cases is much more advanced as a medium than its visual counterpart, as the imagination of one receiver can construe the sounds differently than someone else.

Culture

If there is one thing that's lacking in filmmaking today, it would be culture.

What does this mean? I had many a talk with my friend Lane Leavitt about such, and he pointed out several things. Lane and his wife Debbie Evans are well-known in the stunt community for their riding prowess. Lane and Debbie have trained riders from the *Bourne* to *Fast & Furious* series. The whole family is made up of motorcycle champions.

We've talked many a time of culture and the champion mindset.

One particular movie that comes to mind is the movie *Grand Prix*, Frankenheimer's masterpiece. Made in an era where special effects were not king. It did win an Oscar for editing, but what stood out for me was how Frankenheimer shot the races. Each race was masterfully and uniquely shot. In other words, there wasn't a style or theme for the entire movie, which is not as common in our current age.

Lane brought up this precise observation, and pointed out how the two champs interacted at the very end of the movie. Nothing was actually said, but it was the subtleties that the director and actors used. That was culture. Things that are not *said* are still *communicated*, and it doesn't matter if you are in front of the camera or behind it.

When Anthony Hopkins was on top of his game in *Remains of the Day*, I recall Anthony responding with only a gesture, a slight movement of one of his eyebrows. That was his only choice, since he was a butler and in aristocratic groups, the help are not allowed to speak freely. I'm emphasizing the subtlest points and willing to bet that eyebrow raise encompasses the butler life/culture.

With Steve McQueen/Peter Yates' movie *Bullitt*, it was the good guy chasing the bad guy using cars that created a new culture. The timing was perfect. Despite being out of continuity with the Volkswagen bug, white Camaro etc., it's regarded as the original car chase. The thing that really stands out for me now, all these years, is that it's not flamboyant. Just good ol' fashioned filmmaking.

Note: *Bullitt* is considered the movie with the first car chase. In reality, that was *Thunder Road* with Robert Mitchum.

Let me explain what stands out for me in *Bullitt*. The cars were the perfect choice at the time, not necessarily for the looks, but let's face it, those two cars became iconic after the fact. It was the big wooden steering wheel, it was the lack of power steering, it was revving the engine so as to reach the right power band, and it was all of that being done simultaneously. At that time frame, engine building, by way of porting and polishing* was very common, which gave engines a throaty sound. So, as a result the actor didn't have to act, he just had to drive. Key.

Nowadays, cars are very efficient, and realistically you don't have to put that much effort to get a burn out (burn rubber and create smoke). A remake of the famous *Bullitt* scene was done for the show *Alcatraz*. They used modern Mustangs followed by the ultimate arm, and the scene had some great shots, but the

* Porting and polishing was a common practice in the 1960-70s for increasing power to engines. Essentially, the idea was expanding the size of the valves (porting) and making them smoother (polishing) so the air & fuel could flow better and faster.

filming was effortless. Now, the actors have to "act," and boy, did they.

I personally feel Bill Hickman and Carey Loftin were responsible for putting culture in *Bullitt*, *The Seven-Ups*, *Vanishing Point* and *The French Connection*. All legendary Hollywood movies in their own right. If you watch these movies, you will see a different flavor in each of them.

Note: I will go into great detail about shooting cars in the "Car Stunts" chapter.

Bill Hickman's background was as a driver. In fact, he drove for James Dean back in the day. I have extensive experience driving at high speeds on city streets, and what I can tell you is that they did get the culture right. I've written a book on driving called "The Unknown Art of Driving". (Note: A revised international version is being planned for 2019.)

There's Hollywood in there, but there are guts in there as well.

Moreover, how the cars were set up is worthy of note, but again this will be discussed in great detail in a later chapter.

Obviously, it's the responsibility of the stunt driver to over-embellish some of the moves so as to create the illusion that at certain moments the car is losing control. Not all stunt people subscribe to this, but they have to answer to the stunt coordinator and director.

Stunt people know culture *especially* if they come from that field. Steve Hart, ex-fighter, Garrett Warren, ex-fighter, John Kreng ex-fighter… I could go on. These guys not only have an extensive background in fighting, but also are filmmakers. *We can talk about the details…*

Let's talk about the French, every American's favorite past time. All kidding aside, in terms of cars, driving and filmmaking, the French are further ahead of the game just for the fact that racing has been instilled from a very early age. This is the same with hockey in Canada, football in Texas, soccer in Brazil or Italy.

Just as the French are passionate about car racing, the filmmakers of Hong Kong are fanatical about fighting. Hence the name "Hong-Kong-style fighting." It's totally agreed-upon, by the society or culture, to put more emphasis on the fighting. In some cases, they will spend a couple of months on one fight sequence! In the U.S., a fight sequence gets maybe two or three hours. When people go to the movies in Hong Kong, they may go just for the work of the fight director who, in some cases, has equal billing with the director.

Movies like *Crouching Tiger Hidden Dragon*, *Hard Boiled*, and my personal favorite, *Hero/Fearless* with Jet Li are memorable masterpieces on so many levels. Their passion is deeply rooted. The filmmakers are very involved in their country's culture and it directly reflects in the work.

A visit a few years ago to the Stanley Kubrick exhibit at the LACMA museum was amazingly eye-opening. One of the things that stood out for me was his library of Napoleon. I believe it was a passion of his to shoot a movie about Napoleon, which was in the making for thirty years! He had amassed a great deal of books and probably had a pretty good idea of what made Napoleon tick. I'm not sure if he had taken the time to immerse himself in the footsteps of Napoleon, but he certainly took preparatory steps to understand him.

Writers like Oliver Stone, who wrote *Scarface* and *Midnight Express* immersed themselves in that culture. Yes, Stone was hanging out with drug lords! Stone, a decorated soldier from the Vietnam War, was more than likely not shy of getting into certain areas. After all, a tour of duty in Vietnam kind of makes other environments look like Disneyland. There is someone who really wants to understand the culture and put out realism. And writing is key…

I have the deepest respect for someone who would put his or her life on the line to get you the ultimate story.

Another great example of culture is his work on *Any Given Sunday*. This starts with the second unit director, Allan Graf, who played in the NFL. Jim Brown, Dick Butkus and Lawrence Taylor are all in the film. Do you think they had any influence on the game and shooting? These were legends who changed football! I'm willing to bet that the little details were conveyed in the filming process. And let's not forget that Stone put his crew together for a reason. There is plenty of culture in that film. The second unit shots were so viscerally spectacular. You felt what it was like being on the offensive and defensive lines, and the style of shooting went right along with it.

Life is not lived in an ivory tower… it's being in the trenches. And any one of those men could you tell you many tales.

Conversely, if you are one who researches stuff on the 'net, and won't go to the places or experience life, well, I suggest you throw in the towel, because you'll be doing us a favor. My time is too valuable.

This business is 110%, 24/7, 365 days a year.

The ones who put it on the line are the ones who get ahead, and who most certainly get my respect.

Conflict/High-Risk Areas

Shooting in conflict zones and in high-risk areas takes a little preparation so as to not get into a jam.

I recall a friend telling me about a movie many years ago, I believe it was a Rutger Hauer flick. His modus operandi (M.O.) was the four Ps: proper preparation prevents problems.

In first-unit (main unit) shooting, your first AC (assistant camera), camera operator and DP do a tech check of the equipment. In these risky areas, the requirements, depending on the shoot and locale, may dictate the exact right equipment. For example, you have to consider equipment in the Congo versus the Artic, versus a typical shoot where craft services is less than 100 feet away. Weather, humidity, gunfire, mountains, desert/sand, altitude and so on should have a factor in your determination of your equipment.

A veteran of any of these areas will know the ins and outs of such spots. For example, in a jungle or desert setting with a backpack, with hot and humid conditions, you are looking at burning 10,000 calories a day, easily. So, another preparatory step, in my opinion, unless you are truly conditioned, is too pack on some body fat. Your six-pack won't be any help if you get sick.

If you are ascending Everest, this may encompass training at high altitudes "locally" for altitude simulations, and possibly rehearsing in a restaurant walk-in fridge for cold to get used to changing equipment efficiently.

As I mentioned, my father was a Frogman (a precursor to Navy Seals) in the Portuguese military.

He came from a tropical island off the coast of Portugal. He and his friend had joined the military to become fighter pilots, but while pulling heavy G's in their training, he would black out, whereas his friend did not.

As an aside, his friend had a long career in the military, and I can recall my father telling me that his friend had been shot down five times in the Angola war... and lived!

My father had already been diving professionally with twin tanks and had plenty of experience. At the time, though, he was spending a lot of time underwater but wasn't spending the same amount of time in the decompression chamber, which is necessary. As a result, one time, he had come out of the decompression chamber and was walking at a 45-degree angle! Funky stuff if you don't follow protocol.

There **is** protocol for everything, especially if it's systematic and dangerous.

One of the drills he had to do was to go on a little boat, not much bigger than a zodiac, and throw off all his equipment, then wait 15 seconds and proceed to go after it. This was in the middle of the Atlantic Ocean. My father was a *very* humble man, and I recall only two or three times when he tooted his horn just a tad. One example of this was when he claimed that he didn't have much of a problem doing that drill.

As, a kid he had trained me to swim, but it wasn't like a typical kid where he would get me to swim across the pool. Nope, it was diving for bricks. By the time I was six or seven, I could hold my breath for a couple of minutes. I don't think I hit the three-minute mark until I was twelve or thirteen, when I had grown enough and had the lung capacity.

You are probably wondering what this has to do conflict areas. Two words: skills and guts.

You can't be some skinny jeans slacker and go off to a hardcore area. It would be best to have some foundational training, or someone in the group who does and can offer help, experience or support.

Some of this training should have been started a long time ago, as opposed to "I'm going to do this shoot in two weeks, because of _____." That approach lacks the experience and acumen necessary for the respect due to these environments.

There are several schools of thought in terms of protection. You can hire some "protection," as in those bad ass mofos with some serious firepower, *or* you can blend in. That means if you are from the U.S., it may not be in your favor to wear your Nikes or Yankee's cap. You *truly* need to blend in. Moreover, the thing about serious protection is that you are bringing attention to yourself. A *lot* of it.

The truth of the matter is when you go to a dangerous area, and you can include any poor distressed area, you are seen as a naked man with $100 bills stuck to him! If you are American, there is a good chance they'll bring in the troops and kick some ass, but not always. If you are Canadian, like myself, you are pretty much fucked. The most the Canadians will probably do is send a case of beer and tell them to let him go… eh?!

You want to be prepared!

There are a couple of books I recommend. One is *Dangerous Places* by Robert Young Pelton. The other, by Rosie Garthwaite, *How to Avoid Being Killed in a War Zone* which, in my opinion, is a little more cautious, but has great tips.

These are two schools or training facilities that are used mainly by journalists: https://www.bluemountaingroup.co.uk and http://www.akegroup.com. These are revered as the best schools on the planet for such training. Ex-special forces personnel run them. For the record, they'll spend the first day talking you out of this, so, be prepared.

A friend of mine is the real deal, a conflict/war journalist who has been tortured. He knows the protocols, and it's certainly no joke. There are some truly evil people out there…again, be prepared.

Basics

When going into these areas, it starts as soon as you get off the plane. Customs: did you bring a Carnet or did you bring a DSLR, and are you on holiday? Keep in mind, with the Internet, they can do a Google search if they are suspicious, so be leery of photos on the net or websites and social media, since that might blow your cover.

However, bringing a video camera with a bunch of gear, versus a DSLR, is pretty much a nail in the coffin, and at that point you need to have all the necessary paperwork, including permits and visas.

It's always best to be by-the-book, if you have the budget. If not, and you are savvy to these types of areas, situations and dealing with people, you can rely on some of your own skills. Travelling with a companion of the opposite sex will appease the situation somewhat, for the record.

Don't be surprised that there is a "fee" for God only knows what. Sometimes it's best to just pay them off if it's a nominal fee, and move on. If it's substantial, be cautious not to make a scene, as it can be a detriment. You could play dumb or pull the whole "I'm American, so…" Nope.

If you are a woman, these situations will be compounded, because equal rights are about as common as rainbows and unicorns.

I'm not trying to scare you by any means, but do a little prep.

Once you make it through customs, the pickpockets and spotters are on you. A decoy wallet can be useful. Fill it with outdated credit cards, currencies with large digits, like the Iranian rial, Cambodian riel, Sierra Leonean leone, but if those are not available, dinars and rupees are available everywhere. Make sure to have a mainstay currency, like U.S./Canadian dollars or euros, tucked or sewn in various places, not just in a money belt. That's a rookie move.

Once you are at the hotel, I'd work out from there, in concentric circles, so to speak, since you don't want to get sick eating too far out. Observe the lay of the land, if possible. If you are a little more adventurous don't be going out and getting drunk. Drink at the hotel bar, for starters, if need be.

I found it can take three to five days for the locals to open up to you, but that doesn't mean that you aren't being watched. Some guests may leave and come back at different times from the hotel so as to not have regularity in their schedule.

Don't be surprised if someone goes through your stuff. Some of these places are lawless.

Now, you are ready to go out there and shoot?

Do you have a fixer? How did you find that fixer? Did he have references that you could corroborate? Or does he work for the local crooks? I like a paper trail, so to speak, even if it's somebody from LinkedIn, LightStalkers or CouchSurfing.

A documentary I saw a few years back had a local celebrity as a fixer. He was a reporter for a local television station. The good thing about that was that he could open a lot of doors. The bad thing was that everyone knew him, and he had to sign autographs, and that slowed them down in some cases. Conversely, a beautiful, pleasant or "healthy" looking woman can open doors without too many problems in some scenarios.

Ideally, you want someone who knows the area, the ins and outs, times, and schedules. Preferably, you want someone who has a background with filming, as there's a good chance they will have experienced these things themselves.

Ultimately, you want to be smart, and of course cool. People say "common sense," but these things aren't really that common to be honest, especially if you are coming from a first-world nation.

Of course circumstances change, and then you are left with a decision, and both options are bad, but one is less bad.

In the documentary with the celebrity fixer, the filmmakers were waiting on some mopeds to go into the jungle, which were supposed to come in the morning so they could make it before nightfall. The mopeds came at night, so the filmmakers had to travel by night. They had already paid for the mopeds in advance, which was their first mistake. Second, they went into the jungle in the dark with absolutely no lights. There were two groups of rebels that they had to pass through. They could've been hacked to pieces and never been found, not to mention they were going to see a dictator who wasn't known for being benevolent.

The fellow who came with the mopeds made a scene, and so they felt obligated. That's a *huge red flag*, and personally, I would've walked away. Your life has value. Even worse, there could be no shooting, because the humidity/heat was so thick that nothing could be filmed. I'm sure they knew what they were getting into, but there are times when you need to take a step back. As far as I am concerned, that was a naive move on the producer's part.

This is just an example of one area. If you are in a Muslim country, or a Communist country there may be other pitfalls to be aware of.

One tip that I can recommend is to have a Twitter or email account, so that if you get kidnapped, and have a signal, you can send out a blast to friends and reporters. I personally have the contact information of over 100 reporters from the *Washington Post* and *L.A. Times*. I got the idea from a young man who got kidnapped and was thrown into a trunk, but just before, caught a glimpse of the car and license plate. It saved his life.

Shooting Protests

A lot of principles of shooting conflict areas apply to shooting protests. However, in a "civilized" world, this can still be harsh and deadly nevertheless.

A great primer for this sort of thing is the following article: http://gizmodo.com/5853582/how-to-be-a-citizen-journalist-without-getting-killed. For the most part, I agree with this article. A few things I'd like to add:

Go easy at first. Try to go to less controversial protests at first to get the lay of the land. If it is something in the news 24/7, that's hot news and it might not be best for your first outing. After you've gone to a few protests, you'll see what you really need to bring along. I would always travel light.

Moreover, when assessing the situation, it may be best to see how things are laid out. Are you being bottlenecked into an area, or is it an open field? Options are great when things go down.

A few years back, I taped a Palestinian/Israeli protest. The way the police executed their intervention was brilliant. One tool the police use is horses. Yes, horses. If there is a mob building up... just riding, gingerly, through a group will separate them. Not to mention they are at a higher vantage point and can give you a whack, if need be. And there is nothing you can do because of the mass of the horse. While this is going on, police are standing at a certain distance from each other on both sides of the groups. Then there are the police on bicycles moving at a different rate. There's usually a suburban with tinted windows taking photographs, and don't forget snipers on top of the buildings.

During this particular event there was group of young men gathering. They started to walk/march toward the lights to cross the street. The bicycle police were on it, just following them, hanging back somewhat. As the group crossed the street, the bike cops moved closer. As they approached the opposing group, the police on horses moved in. Within 100-200 feet of the opposing group, the police were able to stop anything from ensuing. The only thing that happened was some hurt feelings.

For press at protests, there is usually an allocated space that may be used depending on the severity or environment. A tip, even if you aren't part of the press, it may be in your best interest to make a pass, even it is bogus. Spend $20-$30 on it. It could be the difference between getting clubbed and not.

This goes without saying, but I'm going to say it. It's great to be young and stick it to the man. However, being drunk or high or unfit will exacerbate a situation quickly. You have to bring your A game for these events. Not to mention it's unprofessional.

You need to be aware enough to predict movements.

Doing this in a foreign land with fewer rights amplifies the situation.

Deceptiveness

Roughly a decade ago, I moved to the South Bay, and I can recall talking to this fellow who took 911 calls. I told him that I had recently moved. He responded, "dude, you are not going to like it there." I asked why. "It's nice." He claimed that people are nuts, and that they'll call the police if they see somebody walking down the street. This intrigued me.

He summarized for me the average call.
Caller: I would like to make a report.
911: OK, go ahead.
Caller: There's a man just who walked by who didn't look right.
911: Has he done anything?
Caller: No, but it may best to send a police officer over to investigate.
911: Has there been an actual crime committed?
Caller: (getting mad) I am older and feel threatened and pay taxes and I don't feel comfortable now! (Something to that effect.)
911: OK ma'am. I'll relay this to my supervisor and see what we can do.

The 911 operator said he didn't like Manhattan Beach, but he liked the Hawthorne calls, as sometimes there were gunshots in the background! This had me howling.

Since I've been in South Bay, I've had a gun put in my face. This was when I was pulled over by the police while riding my bicycle without a light. Multiple times, the police have come over to my domicile because someone said I was working on my vehicle, and I've been followed seven or eight times but have never been pulled over. I tend to walk to and from the beach, but try to get back before 9pm so as to not get hassled by the cops.

A couple years back, a teenage girl heard a noise in the house and called 911. Seven cop cars were there in three minutes, guns drawn, doors open in the middle of the street.

Two years ago, a criminal stole "something" from someone at the Target in Manhattan Beach. Because of this "crime" they had three police forces involved: Manhattan, El Segundo and Redondo Beach. A helicopter was after the "assailant." The news came out with their own helicopter. You would think they were after Osama bin Laden! People were up in arms about that, and they said Manhattan Beach had fallen; emails were circulating in the neighborhood: people felt unsafe. All in all, that search probably cost *at least* $250,000. And for what? When the paper was released, there was no mention of the value of the lost item. This is a travesty, but it *is* the status quo there.

About 4 or 5 years ago, I went to the annual community meeting with the police. I needed an idea of their headspace. A discussion was based on the costs of homes. There was a transition coming with the jails, due to government budgets. The jails were

87% overfilled, so they have been releasing people convicted of low-level crimes for the past two years. In the last two years, in the City of Manhattan Beach, we have had twenty-six crimes, and only one that I would consider violent. Two men made an attempt to rob a Pier 1 store. I wonder how many people who shop at Pier 1 pay with cash? Anyhow…

So, the basis for this meeting was an article that said Manhattan Beach has the second highest price of homes in California, so obviously, they felt that all the newly released criminals were coming there, and the police were informing us of what they were preparing "us" for. At the time, we had 487 block captains. There aren't even 487 blocks in Manhattan Beach!

I really could go on, but what I'm trying to enlighten here is that a "nice" place may not be entirely nice. Be aware that it can actually be dangerous.

By the way, Manhattan Beach has its own SWAT team *and* its own tank. Further, the motorcycle cops ride their motorcycles on the strand with their semi-automatic AR-15s! You never know when some errant volleyball match will get out of hand. Geez.

Conversely, I tutored kids for six months in Compton without feeling anything remotely as dangerous. I have a friend who manages a store out there, and we would meet up for lunch every so often. Each time I go out there, people open the door for me, call me "sir," I always get great customer service. I doubt Compton will ever be referred to as "nice," but at least I know where I stand. If they know you are cool then you are fine… be aware when you are in some "nice place," and you don't know the rules.

The idle rich can be insane. If you ever want to see how these people think or operate, go to a City Hall meeting, and bring some popcorn.

Essentially what you are trying to achieve here is predictability, and your estimation of effort. If it is not adequate or appropriate for the circumstances, things can go south quickly. It's up to you how you go about it to get certainty on the subject or locale.

Surf's up!

Car Stunts

If there is one thing I know, it is cars and what sells, so to speak.

Pretty much ever since I was baby, I've been involved with speed, driving and cars.

My mother said the first time I "stole" the car was at the age of two. My earliest recollections are of my father racing in and out of traffic trying to beat the train with me standing on the seat, just tall enough to see over the dash. Yup, the ultimate in parenting.

My mother said when my father came over to Canada, he was basically working to pay off speeding tickets. They left Europe in the late 1960s, and at the time there really weren't speed limits there. He had a background in rally racing, and finished overall in third place in what is now the world rally championship with the original Mini Cooper. I used to have a framed picture of him receiving his trophy. Then cancer got him and it wasn't pretty. I keep his obituary in the same frame.

It has always been my belief that you can fall from grace, and when it's your time, it's your time. So, you might as well go for it *now*! I have always been proud of my father... I can't say that he taught that me that much, but he certainly inspired me from an early age, and by the day I turned sixteen, I was ready to go...

I have pushed the limits of realistic driving by way of street racing for almost twenty years, and there are certain opinions I have garnered because of it. I touched upon certain scenes like the ones from *Bullitt* and *Quantum of Solace*, but I want to go over some other aspects that make up a scene.

What I want to convey in shooting car stunts is believability as opposed to "look at my stuff." It doesn't always have to flash to get respect from the viewer or your peers. One of the best car chases of recent times was in *Safe House* (Alexander Witt's creation; he did *Skyfall* as well).

The thing about that sequence – and it was the first time I had seen this – I couldn't predict what was going to happen next, and ultimately, if you can do that and keep the audience in suspense, or even better, at the edge of their seat, you've got something.

In shooting *Ronin*, Frankenheimer's use of 300 rally drivers was a testament to his vision. And seeing De Niro look like he was going to hurl was worth the price of admission! You see, they had rigged it so the driver was on the passenger side, and Ol' Bobby boy was just pretending. The driver made him look good, sort of.

First things first: the camera car driver makes the shot. A stunt driver knows *where* to find the camera, but it's the camera car driver that is the glue that makes the sequence. Personally I feel these guys don't get enough credit. If you are looking for a stunt driver, especially a veteran, he'll get you what you want, and even if you don't have a good camera car driver.

Remember in an earlier chapter, where I talked about using the talent as the tool? So, do you have a drifter, a rally driver, or a stunt driver? All of them will create a different feel, in the end. Moreover, I'm sure there are a few guys out there who can do everything, but they may cost you.

Some of the most memorable car chase scenes have been shot outside of the U.S., especially in recent years. There are some freedoms in other countries where there aren't as many restrictions, and the masters can do their "stuff." As time has gone on, laws, rules etc. have put a damper on things. Luckily, Hollywood is a master of illusions.

In the old days, they would rip out the passenger seat, set up a wooden plate and mount a camera, like they did in *Bullitt* and *The French Connection*. Nowadays, you can use an ultimate/Russian arm to follow the vehicle at competent speeds. That's nice if you have the budget to afford it.

The truth of the matter is that the vehicles are not the end-all or be-all. They are an instrument, albeit a pretty cool one. Before I get into this I want to go over some basic things.

There are different ways of showing speed. Anthony Dod Mantle (DP) of Ron *Howard's Rush* refused to use the ultimate/Russian arm, because of the way it looked and felt. You may disagree, but at least he knew why he didn't want to use it.

In *The Seven-Ups* with Roy Schneider, there was a terrific car chase scene, a ten-minute display of all-out, with 70s technology. Look at this scene in the concept of speed and danger. For one thing, you can show speed by showing the hero car passing other cars. If the other cars are not moving as fast, it makes the stunt driver look faster. You don't need speed to *show* speed.

The other part of this scene, and this is *not* used as much anymore as we don't have big boats for cars, *is the suspension*. Those big cars couldn't handle worth beans! What was conveyed was speed because of the suspension travel. You get the idea? They didn't have to "act" by overdramatizing the shots.

Further, the tires were basic, and probably bias ply tires, the big thing back then. They still blew…the technology back then was archaic, but they made movie magic.

It's not about speed…it's about *the illusion of speed.*

Second: you, as the operator, director, DP, producer… there are three ways to get a shot. After all, these are *motion* pictures. You have to have motion! In the above example, the suspension was the motion and it simulated speed.

So, what the hell does that mean? When can you be "crafty" and put your GoPro in the front of your car and get a shot? Or, as the case is now, you can put multiple cameras up with the hopes of getting a shot. That's not film making. That's luck, at best.

You can shoot from a static position - handheld, tripod (sticks), crane, etc. - and have the motion go by. Another way is just place a camera static in a key spot, like they did in the olden days with the passenger seat. And lastly, you can be in motion while the other vehicles are in motion, as well.

It's the artist's vision that defines how he or she goes about it and makes it interesting! This is part of action design.

A recent shoot of a car in the Pikes Peak race had multiple cameras, but not *one* exciting shot! And the funny thing was that it's almost the same length as the car chase scene in the *The Seven-Ups*. Did you say this is an apples-to-oranges comparison? Maybe, but not for me.

One camera could be placed where the pedals lay to show the driver shifting, another for hand shifting, then a shot of the tach/speed, then a shot of a rooster tail of gravel, etc. Alternating those shots and changing some frame rates, maybe the placement of the shot, created a narrative. What you saw was the driver starting to shift, intercut with a rooster tail, and a shot of a spectator wowed by his driving prowess, back to him finishing the shift. It doesn't take much... and that's with static placements.

Again in summary, for this step, forward motion is:

- The object/subject is in motion and you are not.
- The object/subject is in motion and you are too.
- The object/subject is in motion but the camera is static.

The difference between the first and last bullet point is that in the first bullet, even though you are not moving...you can move the camera for panning, up and down, etc. The last bullet...it just doesn't move at all.

There isn't anything simpler than that.

And remember, you need to make the shot interesting and exciting!

Something else you can consider, that has been in a bit of debate: taller tires versus low-profile tires.

With taller tires, you can get a bit more of that motion that we spoke about earlier, not as much as in the 1970s, but enough for some subtle motions. With lower-profile tires, the vibrations and dynamics (vibrational harmonics*) change, and the overall shot changes because of it. This was sort of the beginning of the end. Let me explain.

---

* It has to do with waves. It doesn't matter if it's sound, light or mechanical vibrations. There's a certain frequency ... more waves or less waves, or shorter or wider, etc. They have characteristics and they manifest differently.

Taller tires act a little bit like shock absorbers if you will, *while* creating some motion. Low-profile tires may look cooler, but when you place the camera in various spots on the vehicle, the vibration can reach the camera. So, now you have to compensate by using dampening materials either within the car or around the camera.

This is a very similar principle to how cars evolved. Back in the day, with the original Ford GT, which Jackie Stewart made famous, the car was 50-50 weight distributed. Then the Datsun 240 Z and the perennial BMW came along. As time went on, they made the engines more powerful and changed dimensions, so now they had to compensate for these increases. The result is, for the lack of a better word, that more "stuff" isn't necessarily better.

The same can be said of cameras and shooting sheet metal...

A perfect example of this. I did a few years back by strapping a dolly mount (microdolly) on the front of my hood and placing my camera on it. I was driving a 1999 Grand Cherokee with 140,000 miles on it and a *really* bad suspension. I drove it down a steep hill with curves, chasing motorcycles while I was operating the camera. You don't need the ultimate arm. You need sound driving skills and very good understanding of physics. It was a piece of cake. Note: driving up is much easier, but it doesn't make for exciting content.

Everything was against me, the old vehicle with bad suspension, lack of a camera operator, since the car was swerving too much, and the weight would've thrown the dynamics off. I could only go down the hill, as the power-to-weight ratio was the only way I could keep up with the riders, which goes against physics, as I was fighting some of the movements.

DO NOT TRY THIS unless you know the riders are competent. There is no room for error. *Some people can't perform once the camera is turned on.* Stunt or competitive drivers are the best for this, not any other driver/rider. PERIOD!

Having said that, what made that footage good was the taller tires. It made it harder to drive, as there was more slop, but nothing had to be compensated. You get the idea?

Conversely, vibration *can* be your friend…

Depending on the camera and placement of the camera on the vehicle, vibration can be key. A taut suspension, low-profiles tires, a four-cylinder versus eight-cylinder engine, the age of the vehicle and dampening/bushings factors etc. can each dictate vibration.

If you place the camera in the center of the hood or car door versus the edges, you will have a different frequency rate, and as a result, a different look. Or using a steel bumper versus a modern bumper with a sheathing/shell with styrofoam inside of it will also create a different look.

A great example of this is one shoot where we discovered a place on a bumper that was made of steel. The combination of that with the texture of the asphalt made the footage look about 15-20 miles faster.

As I just mentioned, the road, tarmac, or whatever you want to call it, can be another factor and should be considered in your location scout.

New asphalt is very smooth, but sticky, especially in the summer. In the winter, it contracts a little bit, and the contraction factor is dictated by the weather or locale. For example, in southern California it would be different from the northeast, and as a result, the compound used on the road will be created differently.

These are just some determining factors for the shoot, especially if you don't have the talent and budget to do all the things you want. In other words, clever placement of the camera and a creative locale for the road can make up for lack of other things.

Third: make use of what you've got. Don't look at the way things should be. See the way things are and make clever use of them. *Camera placement and locale.*

Another factor for speed is a term called "strobing." This can be done with light, fixed items like telephone poles, buildings, etc.

I've mentioned before why the opening sequence of *Quantum of Solace* was exceptional: Dan Bradley maximized what he had.

When going into the tunnel in that sequence, there are openings on the side of the tunnel that act like windows and "strobe" the cars with light. In *Quantum of Solace*, the lighting was just enough that you could see reflected on the side of the car… other cars. I'm not sure if the action director found that location with the tunnel windows or if it was the location manager. That's one factor.

Another was when the cars exited the tunnel, there were no telephone poles. So, you could not gauge speed. And because of that, they could work other illusions.

Another great use of speed is moving the camera forward while the opposing talent is closing in. There's a part in this sequence where the camera on an ultimate arm was moving forward with the stunt car (bad guy), and a truck crashed into the bad guy's car. It looks extremely dramatic, especially with the car. For all I know, the speed of that might have been 20 miles an hour, but because of the tight editing, you don't have time to analyze it. Moreover, per the D.P. and 2nd unit director they experimented heavily with frame rates and shutter speeds. He made it quicker by lowering the frame rate, and hence increasing speed. This is a tool used heavily in Hong-Kong-style filmmaking to increase speed in fight sequences.

So, far, the techniques I've mentioned hasn't cost any extra money. Maybe a little more time on the scout.

Another factor in the illusion of speed: when using telephone poles, it is the size or length of the vehicle that counts, meaning a shorter or smaller car versus a longer car affects the appearance of speed as it travels from point A to point B (from telephone pole to telephone pole).

Obviously, this can apply to buildings as well. In the west coast, in Victorian times, the houses were very narrow to save on taxes. Taxes were structured based on the width of homes. Something to think about when scouting…

If you were to look at this in its most rudimentary form, you would be talking about time. Yes, time.

As I mentioned in an earlier chapter, *your responsibility is to make the shot interesting.* And sometimes having no poles or buildings, like in the desert, makes a scene very boring. You see commercials and music videos that spend money on a helicopter and fancy cars, but have boring background images. All show and no go, so to speak.

Further, in these videos, the music becomes limited due to the background. What kind of sounds can you have when essentially there isn't anything going on?

I can recall listening to "British Steel" by Judas Priest and driving up to Mount Whitney. I hadn't heard the album in years and was looking forward to it. When I played it, it just didn't do it justice. The music pace was just too fast for the environment, the high desert.

So, again, when scouting or designing the scene, try to encompass all factors so that it all meshes well. Having quick editing with slow music doesn't *always* work. Maybe in the comedic world. However, the other way does... Something to ponder.

Study this sequence, as pretty much everything in the opening of *Quantum of Solace* was spot-on.

As far as realism, look at *Mission Impossible 2*, especially the car sequence where Tom Cruise is chasing Thandie Newton in the mountains with the Porsche and Audi TT. When losing control of the vehicle, in the spin out, John Woo, a master of slow motion, was able to capture the realism of what happens when things do go out of control and how time stands still. Tommy boy nails it as to what he should be looking at so as to remedy the situation.

Time does slow down when things go out of control, but most people panic and then get killed. An accident is secondary to the actual decision that you are making when things don't go as planned. Meaning, when people are in an accident, at the very moment that it happens, they may have a moment when they decide their fate, despite what's actually going on. Some people may call that a miracle. I call it practice.

These fellows who make it in the industry, stunt people, have repeatedly done things all-out, for many years, and know exactly what's going *on in that moment.*

The cool thing is that when they make it in the film industry, the speeds are sometimes much slower than compared to their driving or riding competition days. So, as a result, it's easier for them to stay cool under pressure.

Here's another point, stunt people can always tell me *exactly* what happens just before the point of impact or just before the accident happens. Whereas "regular" people don't really know what went wrong at the point of impact. It takes a special kind of person to do that. Something to be aware of when casting/crewing up…

Remember, these people put their lives on the line for your viewing pleasure.

If we want to talk about drivers and stunt people, we talk about Gary Powell. I had a chance to talk about racing with Gary a while back, specifically about the Ford Cortina and the Camaro, late 60s and early 70s models. We both understood what that meant: the Camaro's big powerful block engines versus the light, nimble-handling Cortina's. In other words, the Camaro in the straight away and the Cortina in the corners. The whole point of the conversation was that they were neck-and-neck; and that, my friends, is racing. There are no excuses, and what's bigger is not always better. Having structured rules and unlimited budgets makes for boring racing.

If you ever watched any big blockbuster film, you've seen Gary's "driving" prowess. He was the driver who drove a tank in *Golden Eye*, and of course he drove the crane truck in *Terminator 3*. I can't imagine the planning on that piece. It was a train wreck in motion!

The point I'm making is that the use of physics, the overall sense of the dynamics of the vehicles, and the right driver can be the difference between something awesome and a disaster...

Various Stunts

There are various staple stunts to be aware of, as well as some of the pitfalls that go with them.

Fire Burns

There are two common gels that are used for fire burns, one of which is the high-tech compound called rubber cement. Yup, the same thing you used a kid. Slower burn. The others can all be referred to as "stunt gels." Each may have their own proprietary blend, and for the most part can only be gotten by stunt or pyro professionals.

Essentially a few different liquid fuels can be used (lighter fluid, kerosene, gas, which burns the fastest), but the slower the burn, the better.

With rubber cement, the fumes are a little harsh. Something else to factor.

You *definitely* want to have someone who knows what they are doing on this. Standard operating procedure is to have safeties in fire suits standing by with fire extinguishers.

Another factor to be aware of is the clothing that they wear on *top* of the fire-burn suit. Polyester is a no-no, because it can melt into the skin. Cotton or wool is better.

Fire suits have come a long way as of late, as now they have fire suits for women, which for the longest time they didn't.

We have been experimenting with different combinations of materials and such with the top people in the industry. More time to burn means more time to shoot. You have to keep innovating!

Something to be aware of, and this is important. Every so often, the stuntperson while on fire, usually a newbie, just wigs out and will go for the closest person, who is usually the camera operator. A stunt coordinator has told me that on a couple of occasions that he had to tackle a stunt perform to prevent a fiasco.

A recent movie I saw, *Stalingrad*, was shot on the RED camera and in 3D. I saw the fire burn… all the stunt people were lit on fire and that was a sight to be seen! I can't imagine the safety on that…

It's best to use a trained professional for these activities. I can't stress this enough.

High Falls

Another stunt that requires expertise and supervision is a high fall.

Air bags vary in size depending on the height of the fall. However, for the longest time, they used boxes, and to some extent, we still do. A friend of mine did a 150-foot fall onto boxes. Scary stuff.

I believe Bob Brown, an ex-diver, is still king of the high fall. He did a fall of 213 feet… while on fire. Unbelievable! The fact that a human body is capable of such a feat is just amazing. Chatting with Bob, you'll find out very shortly that this isn't something you just do. There were countless years to the point where he got additional training from NASA. Ultimately, the fluid in your brain thickens and as a result stabilizes or enhances your equilibrium. Bob claimed that trampolines are a great tool to develop it.

When Bob does a fall, he measures *everything*… it doesn't matter if it's from a helicopter or a bridge.

Starting out on a trampoline, or a mini trampoline, is a great way to at least develop your micro muscles so that you can get your bearings and be able to function in different or awkward positions *while* in motion.

Boxes that are used for high falls are primarily 24 inches square, and 20 if 24 is not available. There's an exact science as to how the boxes are set up, so please be careful. Pros set the boxes up for Bob, but he still checks and rearranges them to his liking, because after all, it's his life.

Prior to boxes, they used plywood. Yes, plywood. Essentially, it would be two sawhorses with plywood. It wasn't perfect, but it's better than hitting the ground without anything. High-tech stuff, eh?

Air bags have been used since the early 1970s. Bob mentioned Dick Zyker, one of the first to use them. Another name synonymous with high falls is Ronnie Rondell. If you watch *any* action movie from the 1970s to the early 2000s, these were the guys.

In terms of shooting, when jumping off with a camera, I would suggest testing the impact of the camera. Do you want the impact in the back or the side? Unfortunately, manufacturers don't really have a clue with this type of thing, so it's best to create absorption for the camera, or at the very least be aware of the footage in relation the placement of the media on the camera.

I have done 25-30 feet falls while shooting without a problem, which for filmic purposes is plenty to cheat a shot, but I haven't tested all the various cameras.

In *Skyfall*, when Bond gets shot off the train, you will see that sequence is broken down into three shots. You don't need great fall distance for these type of things, if it's done right. This is the method.

I recall my buddy commenting on *Cliffhanger*, where the 30 feet climb was more than the shot & safety called for, but the director insisted. Realistically, 10-20 feet can be used. In the big leagues, or should I say big egos, it's a bit of a different story.

You can be smart about shooting this type of thing. Conversely, using wires versus the free fall can lead to a big difference in the realism. A descender is a device that can allow the actor or stunt person to fall using a wire, but under control. Note: Google "descender, stunt rigging".

A tip: When shooting high falls, you need an indicator as to when the stunt person will jump. Watch the knees…

Fighting

There is certainly a history of onscreen fighting that ranges from Hong Kong style fighting, itself borne out of Chinese Opera and Shaolin warriors, to European style with fencing and sword-fighting, to, of course, good old-fashioned barroom brawls in the U.S. These different fight styles all serve a purpose and have a different history. Each tells a unique story because of their movements.

In a *James Bond* flick, you may see all those backgrounds included in the fight sequences, but in a western, you will see just bar-room fighting, which is "appropriate."

However, this has been changing in the last few years, for example in *Lincoln: Vampire Killer*. The movie had a lot of modern movements, which obviously weren't used back in the day, but movies are changing. And some times these movements will take the audience out of the picture. It doesn't "feel" right.

One thing for sure in terms of shooting fights done with wires: I wouldn't waste too much time rehearsing camera movements on the ground, because as soon as people are elevated, gravity sets in, and depending on where the wires are fixed, there will be an evolution of the choreography. In other words, let the stunt coordinator and fighters work it out first.

I too have some experience with different martial arts, having studied various disciplines and worked with different fighters as well as coordinators who all bring something different to the game. I've learned lots from both Anthony Delongis and John Kreng. Anthony has been inducted into the Black Belt Hall of Fame, and John into the Martial Arts History Museum's Hall of Honor. These are their lives, and they have truly enriched me with their knowledge and experience.

John's book *Fight Choreography: the Art of Non-Verbal Dialogue* is a must for anyone who wants to know everything about fighting. I can't do it justice, it's worth buying!

There are many other things in the action world that are unseen but are of vital importance – namely stunt rigging. *Mad Max: Fury Road* is a masterclass on this art. You can certainly delve into stunt rigging a lot more, it takes hands-on practice, a lot of it. It's an art and a skill unto itself. Ratchets, air ramps, etc. are integral parts of what creates that illusion of filmmaking and exciting footage!

Sports

Sports are an entirely different process when it comes to shooting.

If we are to look at this as a whole, it can encompass a lot of different areas. Action sports organized collegiate leagues, technical improvements for coaches, etc.

I've shot my fair share of college games, especially football. The speed changes with each level. High school versus college versus pro level are exponentially different. My buddy who has shot at the NFL level claims that, "if you see him in the viewfinder... you are already down." That's pretty quick.

When shooting broadcast or sports, ultimately you will be given an area to cover, like the end zone. Word of advice... don't miss the touch down!

With coaching, they are using GoPros on the quarterback to determine what he is doing or seeing. It's key so as to correct things as well as players. Again, knowing where and why to put the camera is more key than just putting "more" cameras on the field.

Hockey uses much fewer cameras than football. If you want to learn how to shoot hockey, CBC Hockey Night in Canada is the standard. It's tradition, and the best display of the game.

As far as making the shots interesting, in terms of action sports, the GoPro has cornered the market. If some of the action sports athletes had cinematography training, their stuff would be on another level! But usually you are awed by the jump, the wipeout, etc. It's the instant gratification of the image. Conversely, some of these people have put lives at stake to pull some of these things off.

X-Games, Red Bull, GoPro have each built an identity and a market. Apply these principles and the work will achieve another level of professionalism.

Previs

Previs, the elephant in the room. What is previs?

Previs is short for "previsualization," the process of visualizing and improving a project before it's actually shot, so as to work out the bugs. In the past, it was storyboards and physical models to help convey the intended final product. With previs, this is done with animation or live action.

Previs can be used for anything from tv to tent-pole movies (big blockbuster movies). Previs can potentially save money in terms of production, as any surprises are worked out beforehand and production doesn't have to adjust during principal shooting. At least, that's the idea. Further, this step can help mold the director's vision.

A good friend, Brian Pohl, spoke at an engagement on behalf of the Global Cinematography Institute and laid out a flow chart detailing previs involvement. Brian was lucky to get out of there alive! (circa 2011). Now it's "generally" accepted.

The truth of the matter is, it's here to stay. There's certainly a fight between cinematographers and previs animators. However, it seems that it has subsided to some degree, especially as of late. There have been improvements in terms of relationships between previs and production. It's a territory issue, which dept gets to control what, and it encompasses the aesthetics of the process.

The long and short of it is that previs and DPs/production need to get along.

Almost 100 years ago, the cinematographer was king. Movies were silent, and cinematographers were heavily relied-upon to create the image. Now, they have lost some market share, so to speak. Personally, I do see value from previs. However, my views on this are from practicality, because tough shots are my specialty.

I recall Brian Pohl telling me about a scene in *Mr. and Mrs. Smith* that takes place in the desert, the one where Brad Pitt and Angelina Jolie discover that they are adversaries. Originally, that was supposed to take place in the mountains. Let's explore this.

Angelinos are quite comfortable in warmer climates, so the desert isn't much of a stretch for them, whereas colder, mountainous environments can create more problems. The originally intended look, from my point of view, could only have been gotten at a high altitude. This would create problems for the crew, not to mention the expenses of transportation and hotels. It adds up. Hence, the sequence takes place in the desert. Conversely, if it had been a crew out of Canada or New Zealand, I would reassess this. Different cooks in the kitchen, so to speak, create a different dish.

I remember coming across what Spielberg did for *War Horse* in terms of previs. When the horse ran through the trenches, it was discovered in previs that the trenches needed to be dug deeper. If this hadn't been discovered in previs, it would have created a serious expense in terms of money and time during the shoot! Previs does serve a purpose, particularly for bigger productions.

For second unit, there are other complexities in terms of movements, and the previs animators would have their work cut out for them; and as result even need experts consulting them.

I have done several previs/second unit shoots. One was on green screen where the stuntwoman was simulated being blown off a ship. Another was simulating a car knocking over parking meters and avoiding a collision. A while back I shot a foot chase sequence culminating in a couple of women jumping on a robber from a building. For big-budget movies, they'll offer previs/storyboard images of the needed shots, like the parking meter sequence. The other previz gigs were created from just script lines or director's notes.

Previs can vary greatly but it's a tremendous help for the director's vision.

Art

There are various forms of art in different media: painting, sculpture, the written word, the visual image (movies), etc. Since this book is primarily about overall production with cinematography and stunts in mind, I'm willing to bet that a cinematographer and stunt coordinator would be able to tell you what *they* think is art. It would make for an interesting conversation.

Within the last forty years, postmodern art has taken shape. I'm not entirely sure what "modern" art was, but I know some classical elements were missing. One is its lack of ability to communicate. In some cases, I believe, there was heavily-consumed LSD. Seriously.

Ultimately, art, regardless of interpretation, has an ability to communicate. And it should be looked upon as such.

Over the last few years, I have been as focused on the arts as on stunts. I frequent museums monthly, and it is now a part of me that should never be neglected.

Before VHS tapes came about, the director would tell the DP/cinematographer to visit a particular piece of art at a museum, as he wanted to have that "look." The cinematographer would spend countless hours studying the piece. Time would be spent looking at the source of the light as well as the quality of the light. Hours, folks…

There is so much to be seen. These masters of fine art were so intricate with their movements that every stroke was an integral part of the piece.

Because I visit museums frequently, when I walk by an art piece quickly, if it catches my eye, it will stop me in my tracks, and I tend to go investigate it. As I mentioned, art is supposed to communicate with you, and sometimes the art communicates with me, sometimes it doesn't. What that means is that *you* have influence as to *how* it communicates. For example, maybe you are having a bad day, maybe you are in love or going through a divorce, etc.

There are certain artists I can really identify with. The artist who really changed my perspective was Edgar Degas. I saw the traditional concept of the "rule of thirds"*.

Degas would paint pictures of women, particularly ballerinas. What stood out for me was that within the frame, some of the people in the composition were cut off, which always made it interesting. You'll find that in a lot of cases, the art is centered, which after walking through a museum, tends to bore me.

Modigliani is another artist who influenced me because of his simple and definite lines.

Van Gogh is another. There are some works that have stopped me in my tracks. The thing about Van Gogh is that he's one of those artists you have to find the right distance to view. If you are a foot too far or too close, it sort of feels out of focus.

Rembrandt and Caravaggio are impressive with their quality and source of light. They are the two main figures in the two most used lighting temperatures, 3200 K and 5600 K, respectively. And we can include Vermeer with respect to using window light.

---

* The rule of thirds is a "rule of thumb" or guideline, which applies to the process of composing visual images such as designs, films, paintings, and photographs.

As you see, the above artists and many more have influenced moving imagery in what we now call movies.

It's another facet with which you can develop your eyes.

Another artist I have tried to understand, feel from, is Picasso, and after a few years, it's starting to come through. The good thing about Picasso is that he was so prolific that when I look at his earlier stuff, I can see how he progressed to his later pieces.

It is similar with Jackson Pollack. To be honest, I always felt that his stuff was a little whacked, but the man was classically trained, and considering his progression and lack of commercial success, he is one of most notable artists of our modern era. I suspect his alcohol-binging and his time receiving Jungian psychoanalysis got the better of him, and as far as I'm concerned that reflected in his work. Oddly enough, though, I do get a feeling of communication despite the spaghetti-looking painting. In other words, there is some definite direction with his paintings. Aesthetics is very interesting in how it affects people.

The above are just some examples on how these particular artists influenced me. And, not so much the little cards that are usually right next to the art. I found that these are full of embellishment and fancy articulation about the work. Let the art speak for itself. If for some strange reason I couldn't relate to it, I would look more intently into the writing. Ultimately, it should be a feeling, and words seem to be a vehicle that don't always do justice.

There have been many forgers, especially in the last forty years, as art is big business. Even the best authorities on the subject have been duped. It makes for good reading, let me tell you. My hunch is that these forgers were not only technically savvy, but their ability to feel was off the charts. The element that was missing in terms of their skill set was originality. Feeling is key.

The above-mentioned true artists had that ability, there were no other influences, sound, moving images, etc., just one image intertwined with their thoughts and the final product.

Another artist of modern day is Errol Morris. The way he shoots, his style, however you want to call it, is full of fascinating choices, and it creates interesting imagery. Most of his documentaries reflect this, and his use of the camera is legendary.

The painters of the past sort of helped define other artists, as each one will have its own effect on me – Cézanne, Matisse, Monet, etc.

In other words, I will read about certain artists and revisit their pieces again and again; and this will help me understand their work. For me, it helps with creating a more interesting image!

I have spent a lot of time in southern France, namely Provence, where Cezanne, Picasso and Van Gogh not only lived but created masterpieces in the area. Seeing where they lived and what they painted gave me an additional understanding of who they were as artists.

Speaking of artists, one thing that I noticed at the Kubrick exhibit was his ability to use the color red. Red, from a filmic/celluloid point of view, can be kind of tricky. His use of it is nothing short of amazing. Red in film would actually bleed into an image, which is something that doesn't happen in the digital world.

Art in its most basic form has been around since early humans and cave paintings. We have always wanted to communicate certain experiences and thoughts.

In Chinese history, during the Fifth Dynasty if I recall correctly, there was a period with a strong influence on art that was originated by the Emperor. The Emperor gave out tools to create art. That period had the least amount of bloodshed, *ever*.

Art has its purpose… and it's something to think about when you think about Hollywood, as Hollywood *is* a business.

Part 3
The Business

Hollywood

There are a lot of talented people here in Hollywood, and equally a lot of untalented people, but that doesn't necessarily mean they won't get ahead. I can recall a survey from some years ago on successful actors, and what caught my eye was that talent ranked fourth in the survey of factors of success.

The "biz," as it is sometimes referred to, is the land of broken dreams or the land of opportunities, depending who has the right attitude and who has been kicked down repeatedly!

The advantage for you is that having read this book, you can bring more commercial value to your work.

Hollywood's paradigm has been in a state of contraction since the loss of DVD sales. Big outfits like Google, Amazon and Netflix smelled blood in the water.

I have been very fortunate to be around people who have been in the business for thirty to forty years or more, which alone is a testament to who these people are. However, there is a real evolution going on. Hollywood is such an influential piece of this interesting planet that this will certainly have repercussions, globally, just like the evolution of the music business at the turn of the 21st century.

Conversely, with evolution, new opportunities arise.

A friend of mine who worked at one of the biggest talent agencies in town, CAA, laid down some simple, mind-blowing facts about what is really going on.

For starters, she explained to me about an amazing actor who can't get work because he doesn't have a "platform," and frankly, he doesn't want to change.

The A-lister's don't need much of a platform, the Tom Cruises and George Clooneys. She also mentioned that their movies don't always make a profit, and that includes some of Mr. Clooney's movies. George has made more money endorsing a particular alcohol brand than from some of his movies.

My friend claimed that the television business was going to revert to the old ways, to the days of the *Dick Van Dyke Show,* where it was the advertisers who basically paid for the shows. With Netflix and Hulu and Amazon and YouTube starting to dominate series or episodic, the networks are losing viewership.

Getting back to the "platform." The people who are not A-list actors, like P. Diddy (Sean Combs) and Jennifer Lopez, create secondary sources of income, i.e., clothing, perfume lines, etc. Essentially, the platform is meant to keep their statistics or popularity up.

You see, CAA hires "artistically-inclined" people with MBAs from big-name schools, and all they do, 24/7, is monitor people's followers, likes and subscriptions, because ultimately they can convert that into money.

They had taken on the Gangnam fellow when he was at 500 million hits on YouTube, and he proceeded to reach a billion hits in no time. The agency figured that they could convert that monetarily, but when he doesn't hold up "his" share, they'll drop him like fourth period Latin!

The people who work in the studio system are no different. Some of them came right out of business school, as opposed to coming up the ranks , folks who know and love the art of making film. It's no longer about that. Nope, it's based on algorithms. The studio paradigm is showing its weak areas.

However, Netflix is benefitting from this, and since they have DVD rentals as well as the ability to stream their shows and movies, they are ahead of their Hollywood counterparts.

Side note: Originally Netflix, based on their understandings of algorithms, came up with this formula by having the "right" director and actor. The last couple of years doesn't seem to reflect that as the quality of the Netflix originals has gone down, considerably.

This is a basic definition of what an algorithm is, per the Cambridge dictionary: a set of mathematical instructions that must be followed in a fixed order, and that, especially if given to a computer, will help to calculate an answer to a mathematical problem.

The truth of the matter is there are over thirty types of algorithms for success, and within those structures there are some other subsets of mathematical formulations.

I remember getting really involved with them, and even found Sergei Brin's (one of the co-creators of Google) computer science paper on how Google was developed. It was in its infancy from what I can recall, but nevertheless, it was interesting and certainly molded how I look at certain things, mathematically.

The problem with math is that it's math, and not art. People don't want to see a visual creation of the result of a problem being solved, and if the "blockbuster" movie flops, it is an indication of exactly that.

From a cog in the machine, there are so many parts of the business, it would be better if, instead of making one $200 million movie, you make ten $20 million movies. If the big studios do it, you'll have a lot more work going on, not to mention the audience will have more movies to choose from. I'm sure there are other factors at play that I may not be aware of, but it worked for many years prior to this current age.

However, depending on who your followers are and the number of them, you can make inroads into bigger projects, which is totally in your favor, and the younger generation understands that and has had considerable success with it.

In fact, networks are trying to get these people on their shows because if some person has 20 million followers, the network gets a higher Nielson rating. Get the idea?

A producer at a talk I went to recently said something very interesting about the independent film world. These people have been hit just as hard. First-time directors used to get twenty million dollars, and now they get twenty thousand, two hundred thousand if they are lucky! What she claimed was that indie filmmakers assumed if they make a film, people will come. What she figured should've been done was to cultivate an audience first. I agree.

A few young men who wanted to show each other something they shot, silly stuff, are the creators of YouTube. One YouTube star now has 20 million followers. He figures that if just one percent of his followers each crowdfunded a dollar, he would have $200,000 to make movie. Then he would sell the film back to them for another dollar, profiting $200,000. That was last year. He's on his third feature film... He doesn't need to wait for the studios to greenlight his films. He has enough followers to be totally independent.

Kickstarter was the same. Five or six young guys wanted to raise money from their friends. Well, it became popular too and just took off. Good for them. Technically, they outsmarted the elite of Hollywood. And it's another confirmation that there is no one right way.

If you are one of the lucky ones who make it and stay there, good for you, because it doesn't happen overnight. Personally, I don't believe in luck, but you certainly can create opportunities by always showing up and continuing to hone your craft, because after all, these are the best artisans on the planet. Hollywood is still regarded as the mecca of filmmaking despite the tax incentive locations that are now calling the shots production wise.

From stuntman legend Vic Armstrong: "Often it boils down to being at the right place at the right time, although you need the talent to take advantage of the luck when it presents itself."

The thing about Hollywood, business, whatever… it's all about relationships, developing them.

A good friend of mine, Ronald Vidor, is a man with more IMDB credits then anyone I know. He has great Hollywood stories. Ron passed on to me what his father said on Ron's first day in the business:

"You start off new and even mostly unseasoned in the camera department in this business. Whether you are working your way up the ladder with no knowledge or not, there is a lot to know and even more responsibility, liabilities, and ethics to keep straight.

Regardless, you always start off with 100 percent clientele and contact possibility of working with everyone; there on, with each bridge you burn, each blunder or mistake you make, that is one less person in that 100 percent clientele you will be working with again. Many high-profile seasoned professionals have shaved themselves down to low percent."

Some have managed to blow their whole career in their first few jobs... something to remember! These are some serious words of wisdom. Try to work out your differences so that bridges never get burned. Truthfully, this wisdom applies to everything, it doesn't matter what type of business or cog.

People generally want to work with people they like *and* trust.

I was very fortunate to be mentored by a well-known cinematographer who is all class. He would introduce me to everyone and so on. On a separate occasion, I went out on my own to "network," and it was a rude awakening. People drinking, exchanging business cards and "yeah, let's make that movie." Spare me. There is *no* way that's going to ever happen, welcome to flake central. This business is not about hanging out and drinking... it's about being in the trenches and finding *and* working with people who are on the same page as you. There are plenty of filmmakers who are in it for the long haul, and it doesn't take long to find out their level of commitment. This business is 24/7, 365 days of the year.

Another factor of this business, and because it seems to be survival of the fittest, you have to reconsider your friends for filmmaking. The truth of the matter is once you figure how hard it is, the quicker you realize your friends are not on the same page, the quicker you'll make progress. You definitely don't want to discourage them, as those friends are golden when times are tough, and it can be very grounding to have them around.

What I am making you aware of is that when you count on your friends to be there and something comes up... that loses the momentum of what you are trying to create. Again, you definitely want these people in your life. All I'm saying is that there is a time for some real conversation as opposed to "what can you do for me." Trust me, that shit gets old. That's why it's so amazing to have veterans who are still good people after all these years.

There is a lot to be learned from veterans, they've been there and they know. They may not know all these new ways of creating a following, but if you've lasted any time in this business they'll always be able to point you in the right direction.

Work hard and keep at it, and the opportunities *will* arise.

Mentoring

Having good mentorship is something of great importance in moving forward in any business or endeavor. Someone who knows the business can guide you away from common pitfalls. Hollywood is full of flakes, wannabes, snakes, but those people are generally not Hollywood.

Then there are the people who *do* make up Hollywood. They love what they do and have worked very hard to get where they are. I have the deepest respect for these people. Some people claim that I give the elders too much respect. Possibly. It's just the way I was raised. There's no right way, but this works for me, and to be honest, I have had access to the greatest minds this great business has to offer, and I believe that's because of my intentions, persistence and approach.

I'm sure you can be slick, have charisma, but ultimately, you should be good at what you do, because when it comes down it, you'll need to deliver.

The old cliché "who you know" does have some credence, and everyone has people that they have worked with and more importantly, trust.

When approaching people to have them mentor you, the top people may not have time, even if you do get access to them. What I found in this business is that *willingness* to help is sometimes senior to rank or popularity or IMDB credits. As you progress in these endeavors, you'll meet people along the way, so it's best to start with someone you can rely on and you can relate to.

There's a good chance something will come up out of the blue and you'll need feedback and guidance, swift and fast; and having a person like this who is just a phone call away is about as good as it gets! Having more of them is even better, as some people have different skills or experiences and are sometimes higher on the food chain.

I've had four main mentors, all of whom I will speak of. Each possesses certain qualities that I needed during my progression for various reasons.

Howard Wexler

First off, I owe my life to this wonderful man. When I leave this world, if I am half the man he is, then I will feel good about myself. This will embarrass him, but as I mentioned earlier about who *is* Hollywood, it is Howard. Let me explain.

Howard is a second-generation filmmaker. His father Sy Wexler was instrumental in bringing film to schools by way of sex education and medical programs. If you went to school from the 1950s to 1980s, either high school or medical school, you saw his films.

Howard started reading cinematography magazines at the age of twelve. Now, with over a hundred feature films to his credit, it's safe to say he knows what he'd doing.

Pretty much on a weekly basis, I have people reach out to me and say that Howard "gave me my first chance," "is the best guy I ever worked with," "taught me everything I know." *All the time.*

There are a few things that I have learned about this business, and I have developed certain qualities, but the one that stands out for me is being humble, because I was as cocky as they came. USC-educated and working multiple decades with the likes of Ansel Adams to Roger Corman, Howard taught me all the basics in the most efficient manner, I might add. There is *no* substitution for experience.

When I started to work for Howard, the conversation would start like this:

HW: Are you available on so and so day?
LR: Yup.
HW: It pays this.
LR: OK, great. What is it?

Note: I didn't ask what the money is first. I just said yes.

HW: It's so and so.
LR: Great.

I would get to the studio and everything was ready to go *and* it was clean. There was no "where is this?" or " should I bring this?" Nope, it was everything and then some. Superlative efficiency and professionalism at its finest.

When I started going on my own, I used this paradigm, and I can confidently say that there are very few people who live up to that standard of professionalism. That's all I know and what I expect. Just knowing this will save you some time.

My progression kind of went like this:

LR: Howard I want to do this.
HW: Well, you can do this or that. … If that is the case… you can try this or that (lots of options that were efficient, cost-effective and added high production value).
LR: Cool. Thanks Howard.

Afterwards…

LR: Howard, um, what did you mean by this and that?

HW: (Patiently repeats it again.)

LR: Oh right. Thanks Howard!

As time went on, and I developed a tendency for second unit and high-risk type of shoots, the conversation changed.

LR: Howard, I want to do this?

HW: Pause. Pause. Bring a medic...

Alex Nicolson

Alex is my trusted old friend and probably without a doubt, the smartest man alive.

I've known Alex for over a dozen years, and sometimes when he tells his stories, I pretty much lose track of time. Sure, Alex has the smarts, to the point that he worked for NASA on various space missions. Some other things he did were help install gas turbines on Indy cars and work on patents for motorcycle simulators. The thing about Alex though, and this is key, is that he never shows how smart he is. He just is. This is crucial when dealing with stunts and dangerous activities, as sometimes there is a lot of testosterone, and that can be your ticket to the afterlife.

What Alex brought to the table was his experience with tolerances. His knowledge base regarding any aspect of physics would put Wikipedia to shame! His latest activity was the recent Mars Rover project for NASA. So I'm sure he can handle various ideas with the tolerances for the type of activities that I wanted to do.

Since you are dealing with speed, mass, tolerances, etc. etc., you NEED TO KNOW what the limitations are! I've never had an accident in part because of these conversations and research.

Lane Leavitt

At a certain point, I had filming experiences that were quite dangerous, but I figured it out myself with the help of Howard and Alex, especially from a cinematographic viewpoint.

But I needed real-world experience, especially in second unit/stunts.

I had come across this fellow by way of an email. I reached out and told him what I was doing and that I'd like to see what he was doing. The fellow was Lane Leavitt, a veteran of over thirty years of the stunt world, and consistently a Taurus winner (Taurus awards are Oscars for stuntpeople). His peers consider Lane an innovator of the stunt world.

With Lane's experiences and mine, we devised new ways to get shots that were interesting, visceral and, more importantly, safe. This is where I learned the importance of a stunt rigger, especially in contrast to a grip.

For first unit, a veteran grip could use a C-47 (a close pin) and flag to make your image pretty. I'm kidding…but a stunt rigger understands tolerances. It's not necessarily meant for looking good, but more so to withstand whatever abuses may occur or its ability to perform a certain act, which ultimately may be factored into someone's life…

I was experienced with high falls/air bags, motorcycles, fire burns, swordplay, fights, etc.. As my understanding came into play, we drilled these skills.

And drilled it again. Over and over You are only as good, or in this case as safe, as your weakest link.

Considering that the second-unit world is quite tough and much more rugged than first unit, Lane is quite soft spoken. However, he does care about his people to the point that every so often he has to read them the riot act. In other words, a good kick in the pants is better when 'practicing' as opposed to when on set. I've learned things in that environment that can't be taught in books... I definitely experimented at Lane's facility and certainly took a few lumps along the way. But it was a space to learn, experiment and innovate. I've always referred to that environment as a "James Bond training camp... but for stunt people." And it was awesome!

David McCullough

In this business, you need more than skills of the craft. You need marketing and your ability to hone what you are about.

I don't think this is so much needed for younger people, and there will be a time when the younger people will have to mentor some old farts, but despite your age, it's about getting yourself out there, and differentiating yourself from the rest of the crowd. Remember, camera operators and stunt people are a dime a dozen in this industry!

In 2008, when the economic crash took place, Hollywood was impacted hard, and there were roughly 15,000 people in my related field playing with their thumbs. At the time, the quickest way to go up the ranks was becoming a Steadicam operator. I didn't have the money for such, and frankly, didn't only want to be a Steadicam guy. Once I knew the basics of operating a camera, I thought of going back to conflict/high risk areas, as most people don't want to do this, and I had life experience.

I recall approaching David Goi, who at the time was the president of the ASC, and asking him if he knew of any outfits for going to such places. The answer was to the effect of, "this is Hollywood, we make that stuff up." This is when I met my dear friend David McCullough. He taught me the importance of developing relationships and honing what skills I had.

When you meet veterans, they'll tell you how they did it, and that is valuable, don't get me wrong, but you may have a completely different skillset or set of circumstances than they did. As I have repeated multiple times, there is no right way, there is only your way.

With David's approach and skills, he was able to point me in the right direction and because of that, build a great foundation for relationships.

These gentlemen are older but don't *ever* get the idea that this means that they are slow. These are some of the sharpest people I know, and they may not tell you if something is bothering them. Trust me.

One time at Lane's place, Lane left for a couple of hours, and the director lost control of the set. It was turning into a clusterfuck. Lane was around for ten minutes near the end, and didn't say anything. I left in a huff. He called me up and listed *every* single person's strengths and weaknesses. Lane had seen *exactly* what had taken place without me even saying a *single* word.

Once at Howard's studio... Howard had rented out his studio for half the day. The filmmakers were in their late 30s, slick, with trophy girlfriends and fancy cars. They had set up the stage with dolly tracks.

Halfway through the shoot, they realized that they had screwed up and had to rearrange the set, including laying the dolly tracks, which would cut into the afternoon.

They approached Howard. Basically, Howard asked a couple of questions, shook his head, and in Howard Wexler fashion said, "may I offer a suggestion?" Howard went back, did a little rummaging here and there, about in about 90 seconds, he had resolved the situation. Everyone was stunned, including myself. I remember saying to Howard "that was AWESOME," and high-fiving him. The point I'm making here is that there is *no* substitution for experience. Period.

The Big Leagues

I have trusted A-listers whom I approach for certain things, but due to their schedules, I only approach them if it is really necessary.

People like Roberto Schaeffer, Garrett Warren, Andy Armstrong, Ray Zimmermann, Gary Powell, Karin Chien have always been there for me, and their experience in the "majors"* has been quite useful. I have also found these people are on another level. You really have to have your shit together for this level: discipline, skill, thick skin, creativity, A-list relationships, etc. etc.

Each one of these people has changed my perspective of the business, because when you are looking up, the business may look like this and that, but looking down from their perspective and experiences, they can paint a clear picture for you. Every one of these people works regularly. On top of that, at that level,

---

* A reference to the Major Leagues, used primarily for baseball.

it's mental, in my humble opinion. These people are smart and tough. Otherwise, you can't last in this business, especially at this level.

Just the stories these guys tell are legendary. Word of advice about dealing with these top-level people: be careful showing off your stories. Their stories are on a whole new level...

Simon Bolivar was a dictator of Bolivia and was considered the liberator of South America. Bolivar never got the same notoriety that Napoleon, Hitler or Genghis Kahn got. However, the story is not about Simon, it's about his wife, Manuela Sainz. You see, she was quite smart, and could've helped Simon with his endeavors. Simon was quite vain, which ended up being his downfall. This is the quintessential example of "behind every great man, there is a great woman."

You are probably wondering what this has to do with the film industry. For these people who end up mentoring you... *you* need to be a Manuela and do what it takes to help them reach *their* goals. You have to *give back*...

Most of these people wouldn't want anything in return, and that is what makes them great people, but from an integrity point of view, you need to. It's your responsibility to flow them power, whichever way they see fit. It may even be a shitty job, but if he or she needs you, you help out. Period.

Having said that, this is something you need to be aware of. People *will* take advantage of you. In some cases, this is called an internship, and in other cases it's some sleazy bastard!

You'll have figure that out, and that can take some time. The truth of the matter is that they know they can take advantage of people, and there are people waiting in line to serve them. It can be part of the process of learning and getting experience.

However, I believe the majority of people just want you to do well, and maybe once you've made it or have some success, you can pass the baton to someone else who could use the help.

I have younger people who reach out to me. Some reach out once and then I never hear from them. Some repeatedly reach out and let me know what they are up to, which is smart. *The thing about the business is that you just have to keep showing up!*

Once you've been in the trenches, you'll have new problems, and you'll get more respect from them.

There's a catch: why should they mentor you?

This is a question you need to ask yourself. I've heard in certain circles that they don't want to mentor anybody because once you know what you are doing, you'll end up leaving and then *competing* against them. This is a valid point. You'll have to find the proper match...

With Howard, because of the path I chose, it was very different, so I don't really compete with him. In fact, when something falls on my plate that I don't want to do or is more suited for his skill set, he's the first person I call. He may say no, but it keeps that exchange up with him, and since he's a good guy, he'll do the same.

In closing, there's something that circulates, in any community, when mentoring is involved: tough love.

Some people believe you have to scare and discourage novices; and overall, just be tough with them.

It doesn't matter if it's Wall Street, politics in Washington D.C. or Hollywood, these places will always be a zoo, but the person you are mentoring will discover these things themselves, without "help" from certain people. They'll eventually figure out whether or not they can cut it. They need guidance and a friend.

The likes of Larry Parker of Mole and Richardson, Ira Tiffen with Schneider Optics, and James Mathers of Digital Cinema Society have helped me out and forwarded my progress and career. They are very wise and have been in the business a long, long time.

There are a lot of good people out there who want to help.

Miles Davis mentored Herbie Hancock. Akira Kurosawa mentored Ron Howard. Both of these guys were already on their way. And it seems that it worked out for the both of them.

There's a great little story that Carmen Appice of Vanilla Fudge shares of this unknown, green drummer. Carmen was a professional drummer who worked with all the best! This unknown drummer claimed that he stole "a" move from Carmen. That drummer was John Bonham of Led Zeppelin. Never underestimate the power of influence.

Lastly, above all, is this: all you do is just put one foot forward, one step at a time...

The Thought Process

What starts before anything in any endeavor or business is a thought, an idea, a concept. In whatever form, something comes in your mind.

With this thought something is born.

You might say that the thought is the kernel that will develop to "something" eventually.

This thought, it has to be brought into the physical world. Words are usually the vehicle.

With that thought, there are certain emotions and actions that come into play. Once that is worked out, the making or creating of the product ensues.

For example, Ferrari. What do you think about when you think about a Ferrari? A sexy, high-priced, well-handling vehicle? I will tell you that that final product was born out of that one thought: sexy and fast. When you decide to make it well-handling and fast, that makes it high-priced.

What about Porsche? A different thought. Enduring, efficient and aerodynamic? At the time when Porsche came onto the scene of LeMans, their engine was half the size of their competitor's, which made the car light and more fuel-efficient.

Lastly, the chief designer for BMW in the early 2000s, Chris Bangle, was instrumental in changing the look of BMW forever. What do you think his thought was? Well, one thing for sure, he no longer felt the tools were adequate for the new designs, so he changed the tools themselves. Profound! He claims that his influence was Bauhaus architecture.

I used cars as an example because it's a three-dimensional item that can be seen or has been seen. How does this apply to filmmaking? Same thing.

Artists and innovators like Sergio Leone, Akira Kurosawa, Dar Robinson, James Cameron, Ferdinand Porsche, Nikola Tesla, Elon Musk, François Truffaut, Michael Jordan, Steve Jobs, Wayne Gretzky, Bruce Lee… all started with *one* thought.

Every one of those people were opposed, heavily, I might add, along the way. Their emotions would run high, and they were all head-strong in their own ways. And you'll have to go through that. Possibly, those emotions come into play when you are trying to figure how to do it. Maybe you have to invent something? Create a new technology? Talk to different people?

At this point you haven't physically done anything, in terms of using materials. So, this planning needs to be worked out. Then there is the effort of putting it together. The final, and probably the hardest stage, and even more so, the very last step *will* be the hardest step. It's the way things work…

Look at the PR campaigns against this fellow, Elon Musk and his Tesla car. This should be used as a textbook case of going up against the status quo or the establishment, pick your poison.

Ultimately the guy has created a vehicle that isn't oil-dependent, and had the highest rating *ever* by Consumer Reports. Ever, people! Do you think the oil or car manufacturers want this guy succeeding?

I can't begin to tell you how many times I've heard Clint Eastwood talking about getting his movies made, and that it barely happened. The guy is an iconoclast! He is one of the few Hollywood directors who come under-budget and under-time. So, it doesn't matter who you are, *someone* will make an attempt to put a stop to your goals and dreams.

Life is not unicorns and rainbows… it's a knife fight with your arms tied behind your back, while somebody does a wet willy[*] in your ear, which is highly annoying! Despite those hurdles, pitfalls and snakes… it comes down to your original idea.

It's up to *you* if you want to have someone else control your destiny.

"The music business is a cruel and shallow money trench, a long plastic hallway where thieves and pimps run free, and good men die like dogs. There's also a negative side." - Hunter S. Thompson.

The film business is not too far away from that…

---

[*] A bully, big brother or good friend wets his finger by putting it his mouth then puts in someone's ear, usually when you are sleeping or in a position where you are defenseless.

You, the Artist

The most important aspect of this book is you. The artist.

The way this book was written was for you to create your *own* point of view, because you will find all kinds of people who will tell you otherwise.

"Be yourself; everyone else is already taken." - Oscar Wilde

Some years ago, I pursued acting. It was why I came to Los Angeles. I had been given a scholarship. Part of the "curriculum" was to read a 200-book list filled with everything from Eisenstein to the Bosnian war. It was deep. Essentially, it was to enlighten you to life in written form, from some of the greatest minds.

Personally, by that time I had covered some of the most dangerous places, people and environments, which I experienced firsthand. But this direction regarding the basics, it was to create *your own* viewpoint.

There is no right or wrong way, despite what the critics may say. I've given you some options, areas to explore and points of view to take a look at. Nothing is written in stone.

There is an evolution with technology as well as business, and it's all changing at break-neck speed.

Hollywood can be very shallow in how they evaluate or see you, but having a good sense of who you are will take you a long way. Marketing and consumerism are taking over. Talent is disappearing, or should I say being ignored, unless you have the "look."

Did you know that Neil Young had polio as a kid and because of it, he walks with a limp? Aretha Franklin was a little on the heavy side. How about Stevie Wonder or Ray Charles with their lack of eyesight? How about Fred Astaire? He was no George Clooney, not to mention he was balding in his prime.

I doubt very much, in these current times, these legends would be given the opportunity because of their outward appearance or "imperfections." It's a shame.

Your viewpoint will be senior to any new camera, fist pump, fad diet, the latest news on TMZ or any other nonsense. Because, in the long run, none of those things will matter. *Be true to yourself.*

The one thing that is lacking in Hollywood/Los Angeles is admiration: the scarcest of all qualities.

Some years ago a friend of mine worked under Jeffrey Katzenberg, one of the founders of DreamWorks. She would tell me how he talked to people. If you were a rocker, he would talk to you to like a rocker; if an executive, he would talk to you like an executive.

I had a conversation with Grace Slick in Austin one night. It was probably one that she had had many times talking about Jim Morrison, Jimi Hendrix, but the conversation was mainly about Mick Jagger. She too explained what my friend said about Katzenberg, because you will meet *all* kinds of personalities, and if you allow them to *be*, you'll have a lot more success.

The director is one of the people who has to have this skill.

If you admire them, they'll be an ally and a friend and be willing to contribute to your creations. Obviously, there may or not be any commercial success with any kind of project, but it's been a useful tip when dealing with people.

It's exhausting trying to get the attention of some executive or someone of importance only to find out that they have *already* heard it before, or even better, you hear in return, "what can you do for me?" That's the way it is, but there are a lot of classy people who will just be cool with you, the artist. This is not about being headstrong or having thick skin, it's about having a great sense of who you are. That is done by *living*.

Hopefully, this book has been some value to you.

Be the best you can be.

Your friend,
Lawrence Ribeiro

About the Author

"Lawrence's personal style combines art with grit." – Adforum

With over 100 action sequences under his belt—from fist fights to car chases—Director and Action Design expert Lawrence Ribeiro works hard to innovate and create new experiences.

His action sequence "The Chase" won 8 Best Action, Best Editing and Best Cinematography Awards. It exemplifies what can be done through raw stunt work, camera movement, locations, sound design, and editing.

For the past three years Lawrence has traveled the world—from Shanghai to Milan to Istanbul. He's fluent with cultures, location design, filming techniques, and advertising creative.

Adforum states, "Lawrence's mission is to educate clients, agencies and production companies about how a combination of the right team and the right techniques can result in genuinely thrilling content that doesn't cost a fortune."

Lawrence is a regular contributor to *BCMA* (Branded Content Marketing Association) and has written for *MovieMaker* and *Filmmaker* magazines. He serves as a finalist judge for the Emmy Awards and the Venice Television Awards.

www.lawrenceribeiro.com

25168928R00122

Made in the USA
San Bernardino, CA
09 February 2019